SCOTTISH
BRANCH LINES

SCOTTISH BRANCH LINES

C.J. Gammell

OPC

Oxford Publishing Co

First published 1999

ISBN 0 86093 540 X

Published by Oxford Publishing Co

an imprint of Ian Allan Publishing Ltd, Terminal House, Shepperton, Surrey TW17 8AS.
Printed by Ian Allan Printing Ltd, Riverdene Business Park, Hersham, Surrey KT12 4RG.

Code: 9903/A3

Front cover:
North British 4-4-0 No 256 *Glen Douglas* work the 1960 Scottish railtour organised by the RCTS and SLS. The engine, built at Cowlairs in 1913 was restored to its original condition. *Author*

Front cover, lower left:
'Jumbo' No 57441 waits at Kirriemuir with a special in June 1960. The branch closed to passengers on 5 August 1952. *Author*

Front cover, lower right:
A Park Royal four-wheeled railbus waits at Craigellachie in July 1959. The railbuses were introduced to the Speyside line in 1958, but only lasted until 1965 when BR withdrew passenger services. *Author*

Back cover:
The Whithorn goods headed by 'Jumbo' No 57340, built at St Rollox in 1892, works the thrice weekly branch freight in August 1960 shortly before closure. *Author*

Title page:
The approach to Peebles on the former Caledonian Railway as seen after the closure of the branch from Symington. The line was closed to passengers in June 1950 and freight from Broughton in June 1954. The connection to Peebles West was in use until 1 August 1959. In this view, taken after the line had closed completely, the CR signals and signalbox are in situ. The ornate station with overall roof can be seen in the distance. Photograph taken on 26 August 1960. *Hugh Ballantyne*

Contents:
Class 2 2-6-0 No 78047 en route to Berwick-upon-Tweed from St Boswells on 21 October 1961 with a single coach train. The line through to Kelso closed to passengers on 15 June 1964. *A. Moyes*

Contents

Introduction

The mileage of Scottish railways was reduced considerably during the postwar period and many scenic lines disappeared from the system for ever. Steam motive power was the dominant force until the 1960s when more modern traction was introduced including various designs of four-wheeled railbus. The experiment was short-lived as modern traction did not save the rural railway. Several lines were considered to be vital in serving the more remote communities in the Highlands but road improvements soon ousted them. However, there is still a system north of Perth which has survived although heavily subsidised. During the period from 1958 to 1966 the preserved Scottish locomotives, the 'Jones Goods', *Gordon Highlander*, *Glen Douglas* and Caledonian No 123 roamed around the country on special tours organised by the railway clubs. Some ingenious railtours ran during the 1960s and the Easter 'Scottish Rambler' railtours were classics in their time.

Today, the situation has stabilised and a basic network of railways survives under ScotRail. Here and there is a poignant reminder of the past, a crumbling embankment or a concrete platform edge on a long forgotten country line reminding us of the once extensive network that covered the whole country.

The Caledonian branch engine was the '439' class 0-4-4T of 1900 built to the McIntosh design and classified '2P' by BR. No 55195 is seen at Killin on 5 May 1959 with the single-coach passenger train to Killin Junction. The line was closed completely on 28 September 1965 following a landslide in Glen Ogle on the former CR route from Callander. *E. Wilmshurst*

Highland

Wick to Lybster (13½ miles)

The line from Wick to Lybster opened to traffic on 1 July 1903 under an Act of 27 November 1899. The railway was built as a light railway and was worked by the Highland, remaining independent until the Grouping. The Wick & Lybster Light Railway was financed by the Government, Caithness County and the Duke of Portland. The W&LLR was absorbed into the LMS in 1923 and had three trains per day for most of its life. There were stations at Thrumster (4¼ miles), Ulbster (7¼ miles), Mid Clyth (9½ miles), Occumster (12¼ miles) and Lybster (13½ miles). The railway had few earthworks and followed the contours of the land. The branch was worked by a Highland 0-4-4 tank, No 53 named *Lybster* by that company and built in 1890 as a saddle tank but rebuilt in 1901 to a conventional side tank. No 53

was renumbered 15050 by the LMS and worked the line until withdrawn in 1929. Drummond 0-4-4Ts Nos 15051 and 15053 (ex-HR Nos 25 and 45 of 1905) worked the line until closure, the branch engine being housed in a small one-road wooden shed at Lybster. From 1921 the HR ran Saturday special trains for drinkers following the closure of public houses by the council in Wick. The impoverished LMS closed the line from 3 April 1944 to all traffic, the stations at Ulbster, Occumster and Lybster being retained as road-served goods depots until February 1951. Today, the station building at Thrumster survives but is out of use. At Ulbster there are traces of the platform and at Mid Clyth there is little trace of the station. At Occumster there are traces of the platform and at Lybster the station building is now a golf clubhouse. The goods shed is still in situ at the latter station.

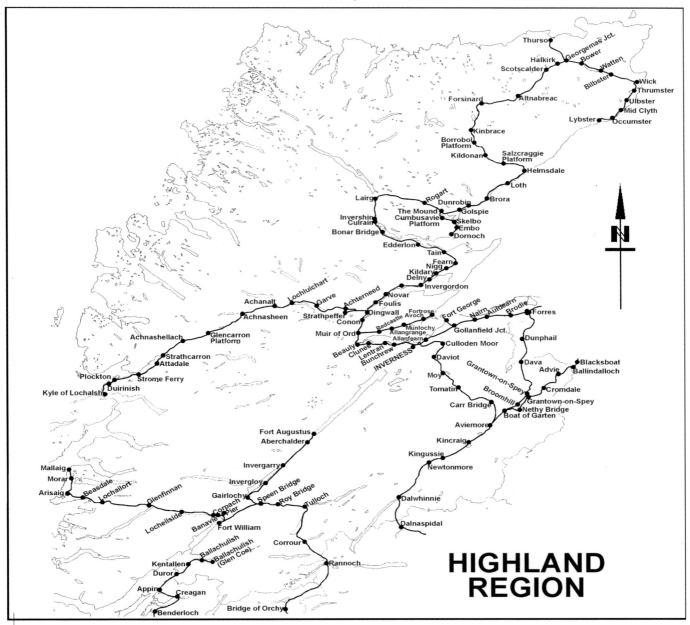

HIGHLAND REGION

VIEW OF LYBSTER STATION

Early scenes on the Lybster branch with the branch train at Lybster station on what looks like the first train with railway staff gathered on the platform. The engine is No 53 *Lybster* dating from 1890, having been rebuilt from a saddle tank in 1901 by the Highland Railway. This engine, an 0-4-4T of Jones origin, worked the line until 1929 when it was withdrawn by the LMS as No 15050. *Lens of Sutton*

The all-timber construction of the terminus at Lybster shortly after opening. The fence is festooned with advertising in true Edwardian fashion. The line was opened as the Wick & Lybster Light Railway on 1 July 1903 and worked by the Highland. The view here is towards the buffer stops with the extensive cattle dock on the left. *Lens of Sutton*

Lybster station in 1912 when the branch was in its heyday with crowds on the platform from the mixed train which consists of ancient HR four-wheeled stock and goods wagons. The single-road shed can be seen in the background. The handbell for announcing departing trains can be seen on the windowsill. *Lens of Sutton*

Georgemas Junction is the junction for the Wick and Thurso lines and sees through trains to both towns. In this view, taken on 14 July 1959, Stanier Class 3 2-6-2T No 40150 is seen on a Thurso train when the line was worked as a branch. *Author*

Wick and Thurso (14½ miles, 6¾ miles)

The 14¼-mile Georgemas Junction to Wick and 6¾-mile stretch to Thurso are not really branch lines in the accepted sense as they are both recipients of a through service from Inverness. The lines are the end of the main line system in Britain. Thurso is the most northerly station in the British Isles, being 721½ miles from Euston. The two lines opened to the public on 28 July 1874 and were worked from the outset by the Highland Railway. Today, both lines form part of the ScotRail network.

LMS 0-4-4T No 15053 was one of the Highland Railway tanks built at Inverness from 1905 to 1906 for use on branch lines. The class of four locomotives lasted through the LMS period and the last two engines survived until 1957. The Dornoch branch saw Nos 55051-55053 in use until 1956, when they were replaced by more modern motive power. *P. Ransome-Wallis*

The Mound to Dornoch (7¾ miles)

The main line opened to Golspie on 13 April 1868 and was worked by the Highland Railway from the start, the Sutherland Railway being absorbed into the Highland in 1884. The Dornoch Light Railway was authorised in August 1896 and opened on 2 June 1902. The Highland Railway worked the branch which was laid out as a light railway but the lightly laid line had crossing gates where it crossed the road. The DLR owned a hotel at Dornoch to cater for visitors to Britain's smallest cathedral 'city'. The Mound, named after Telford's embankment of 1817, catered for the branch with a separate platform situated behind the main line station.

The railway crossed a causeway to Cambusavie Platform (1¼ miles) by the shore of Loch Fleet and was crossed by the road before heading off to Skelbo (3¾ miles), Embo (5 miles) and Dornoch (7¾ miles). Two trains were run on weekdays

and were scheduled as mixed under BR, the frequency being three per weekday under the HR and LMS. Trains were worked by Stroudley 0-6-0T No 56 from the opening but Drummond 0-4-4Ts Nos 45 and 46 worked the line until 1956. These engines, which became BR Nos 55051 and 55053, were the last ex-Highland engines to work. In 1957, a very strange occurrence took place in that a Western Region pannier tank of the '1600' class, No 1646, was brought in, to be followed by No 1649 in 1958. These lightweight engines were highly suitable for lightly laid lines and were new. BR withdrew the service on 13 June 1960 to all traffic but the panniers lingered on to December 1962 as station pilots at Dingwall. On the site of the branch today there is no trace of Cambusavie or Embo but the Embo building is in a nearby field. The platform edge survives at Skelbo and Dornoch has been turned into a retail outlet. The goods yard is now a small industrial estate.

The Mound with an ex-LMS Class 5 4-6-0, No 45319, shunting in the Dornoch bay platform on 1 May 1957. The line to Dornoch, which was worked by Highland Railway 0-4-4Ts until 1956, closed to all traffic on 13 June 1960. The restaurant car from Inverness can be seen in the background. *Hugh Ballantyne*

A passenger's view of The Mound seen from the front of the guard's compartment on 22 July 1955 with Highland 0-4-4T No 55051 crossing the main road. The guard has opened the gate which covers both the road and the railway. *L. Dench*

Left:
Dornoch terminus on 13 July 1959 shows the cramped station layout and the LMS coach used on the mixed train to The Mound. The coal is probably for the loco which at the time was an 0-6-0 pannier tank, No 1649. The branch closed the following year on 13 June 1960. *Author*

Left:
Strathpeffer was a Highland 0-4-4 saddle tank built at Inverness in 1890 for use on the branch. The engine replaced No 12, a Hawthorns 2-2-2 tank of 1862 which lasted until 1898. No 13 was rebuilt as a side tank in 1901 and later used on the Wick & Lybster Light Railway. The engine in its rebuilt form survived under the LMS until 1929. *Locomotive Publishing Co*

Above:
Strathpeffer with LMS Sentinel railcar No 4149 forming the 11.10am from Dingwall on 18 May 1928. The railcar was one of the LMS batch of 12 vehicles introduced in 1927 which lasted until 1935. *H. C. Casserley*

Fodderty Junction to Strathpeffer (2½ miles)

The Kyle of Lochalsh line was opened from Dingwall to Strome Ferry on 19 August 1870 and Strome Ferry to Kyle on 27 June 1892. Due to opposition from landowners, notably Sir William MacKenzie, Strathpeffer was bypassed. The short branch to Strathpeffer was opened on 3 June 1885, having been authorised in July 1884. The line had a fairly frequent service and the Highland Railway opened a hotel in 1911. Mixed trains were run and various Highland Railway locomotive types worked the line including the Drummond

0-4-4T later to become BR No 55051. The LMS introduced a Sentinel railcar experimentally during the 1920s but this had a limited capacity. The LMS Sentinels had a short life with 15 being built during the period 1926 to 1930 including a vehicle jointly owned with the LNER. The LMS withdrew the passenger service from Dingwall to Strathpeffer on 23 February 1946 and BR withdrew the freight traffic from 26 March 1951. The building at Strathpeffer has survived and is now in use as shops for tourists.

Strathpeffer station today has been put to another use and has been well restored. The building houses a tea room and shops selling tourist goods and crafts. *Author*

Muir of Ord to Fortrose (13½ miles)

The railway to Fortrose on the Black Isle was authorised by an Act on 4 July 1890 with the intention to run to Rosemarkie, a distance of 15¾ miles. The line was opened on 1 February 1894 to Fortrose where it terminated, the Rosemarkie extension having been dropped. The terminus at Fortrose was approximately 7½ miles as the crow flies across Inverness Firth to Inverness as against 26¼ miles by rail. The Highland Railway ran four trains per weekday with an additional on Saturdays. The train service was reduced to three under the LMS but the Saturday extra still ran. Stations were provided at Redcastle (3¾ miles), Allangrange (5½ miles), Munlochy (8 miles), Avoch (11¼ miles) and Fortrose (13½ miles). The line was closed to passengers on 1 October 1951 and freight on 13 June 1960. The last train over the branch ran on Tuesday, 14 June 1960 and originated from Aberdeen as part of the SLS/RCTS railtour of Scotland which toured the country from 11 to 18 June. The train left Inverness at 3.50pm with stops at the four intermediate stations. The locomotive was ex-Caledonian Railway 0-6-0 No 57594 of the former '812' class dating from 1899. BR classified the type as '3F' and one member of the class has survived. A footpath runs from Fortrose to Avoch and there is a road from Redcastle to Muir of Ord. The Black Isle nearly had another branch line as the Cromarty Light Railway was authorised on 1 August 1902 from Conon to Cromarty and six miles had been laid by 1914 but the rails were removed for the war effort. Redcastle station building was being restored in 1997 for use as a post office.

Right:
Avoch, on the Black Isle branch on 14 June 1960 with the last train, organised by the SLS and RCTS and hauled by Caledonian 0-6-0 No 57594. The branch closed to passengers on 1 October 1951 and freight on 13 June 1960. Part of the line has been converted into a road. *Author*

Gollanfield Junction to Fort George
(1¾ miles)

The line was authorised on 4 July 1890 and opened to traffic on 1 July 1899. The line terminated at Ardersier which is two miles from the fort. The junction was renamed Gollanfield Junction following the opening of the line and the Highland Railway provided 10 trains per weekday. The LMS withdrew the passenger service on 5 April 1943 and BR the freight on 11 August 1958. The track was lifted shortly afterwards but the goods shed survives at Fort George.

Left:
The SLS/RCTS special as seen at Fortrose behind ex-CR 0-6-0 No 57594 on 14 June 1960. The ex-Caledonian '812' class originated in 1899 and an example of the class, No 828, ex-BR No 57566, can still be seen at work. *Author*

Below left:
Highland motive power included designs by William Stroudley who built 0-6-0 tanks for use on branch lines. Three of these Highland 'Terriers' were built during the period 1869 to 1874 and numbered 49A, 56B and 57B. The engines worked the Fort George, Dornoch and Findhorn lines and lasted until LMS days, the last member of the class being withdrawn in 1932. *Lens of Sutton*

Below:
The 'Jones Goods' passes the site of Gollanfield Junction on 21 April 1962 with a BLS/SLS railtour. In this picture the track to the Fort George branch has just been taken out following the complete closure on 11 August 1958. The LMS had withdrawn the passenger service on 5 April 1943. *Author*

The terminus of the 1¼-mile branch to Fort George was opened by the Highland on 1 July 1899 and was, in fact, in Ardersier, some way short of the town. The passenger service was withdrawn by the LMS in 1943 but freight survived under BR until 1958. The station is seen in BR days when in use for goods only. The goods shed has survived to the present day. *Lens of Sutton*

Aviemore to Forres (35¾ miles)

The original Highland main line from Aviemore to Forres was opened on 3 August 1863 and throughout to Perth on 9 September 1863 under an Act of 1861. There were stations at Boat of Garten (5 miles), Broomhill (8¾ miles), Grantown-on-Spey (12½ miles), Dava (21 miles) and Dunphail (27¼ miles). This route was duplicated when the Highland main line via Slochd Summit was opened throughout in November 1898. BR closed this, the old route, to all traffic on 18 October 1965. Since closure, the Strathspey Railway has reopened the southern end of the line from Aviemore to Boat of Garten with a proposed extension to Grantown. The Strathspey Railway commenced operations from Aviemore (Speyside) to Boat of Garten in 1979. Dunphail and Dava stations are now private houses, Grantown is now an industrial estate and Broomhill has a new building recently erected and lived in by Strathspey Railway staff.

Spean Bridge to Fort Augustus (23 miles)

Promoted locally the Invergarry & Fort Augustus Railway received authorisation on 14 August 1896 to build a line from Spean Bridge to Fort Augustus at the south end of Loch Ness. A railway from Spean Bridge to Inverness by way of the Great Glen had been mooted but the proposal was defeated as the Highland was keen to guard against territory encroachment by

the North British Railway. The I&FAR became a pawn in the battle between the two larger companies and suffered as a result. The line was opened for traffic on 22 July 1903 and worked by the Highland. In 1907 the NBR worked the line but gave up four years later on 31 October 1911. The line was reopened on 1 August 1913 and worked by the NBR again who purchased it in 1914 for £27,000. By 1923 the railway had become an outpost of the LNER which ran the passenger service of four trains per day. The passenger service lasted until 1 December 1933. The LNER then ran a weekly freight on Saturdays until 1 January 1947.

The I&FAR had intermediate stations at Gairlochy (2¾ miles), Invergloy Platform (7½ miles), Invergarry (15 miles), Aberchalder (19½ miles) and Fort Augustus (23 miles). The railway, upon opening, had continued a further ¾-mile to Fort Augustus Pier where a connection was made with McBrayne's steamers, but this arrangement was short-lived and lasted only until 1906. The station platforms were constructed utilising concrete and as a result have survived the rigours of time fairly well. The stations at Gairlochy, Invergarry and Fort Augustus were converted for use as camping hostels by the LNER in prewar years. Today, Gairlochy site is a caravan park. Invergarry has platform remains but nothing is left of the station at Fort Augustus. The trackbed to the pier is now a private road.

Aberchalder station on the former Fort Augustus line was a residence when this photograph was taken on 2 June 1963. When the line closed to passengers in 1933 the LNER turned three of the stations on the branch into holiday homes which were used during the summer months. *Author*

Gairlochy station on the Fort Augustus branch was of the island type with concrete edges to the platform. The line, which was opened in July 1903, had a chequered history and lasted until 1933 to passenger traffic under the LNER. The LNER converted the station into a camping hostel and today the site is a caravan park. *Lens of Sutton*

Fort Augustus station with the opening train on 22 July 1903 with Highland 4-4-0 No 48, built in 1901. The railway did not make much money and the HR gave up working the line in 1907. The NBR purchased the railway in 1914 and the LNER closed it on 1 December 1933 to passengers. Freight trains ran until 1 January 1947. *Macintyre Fort William*

Sixty years later the remains were still visible. The goods and engine sheds in this June 1963 photograph have survived, as well as the lengthy platforms. *Author*

Banavie Junction to Banavie Pier (1¾ miles)

Opened on 1 June 1895 under the WHR Act of 1894, the line was to be extended up the Great Glen but the Highland Railway opposed the projected extension. The branch was operated three times a week according to the 1922 *Bradshaw* but was closed by the LNER to passengers on 4 September 1939. BR withdrew the freight on 6 August 1951. The station is now a private house.

Gondolier and boat train at Banavie Pier, showing NBR No 343 and the steamer side by side. The short branch was opened on 1 June 1895 as part of the West Highland with trains connecting with the steamer service. The LNER closed the line to passengers on 4 September 1939. *Commercial card*

Connel Ferry (Strathclyde) to Ballachulish (27¾ miles)

The Callender & Oban Railway, an independent concern operated by the Caledonian Railway, was opened through to Oban in July 1880. A branch to Ballachulish was sanctioned on 7 August 1896 and completed in 1903. The C&OR had promoted a line through to Fort William in 1895 but the bill was rejected by Parliament. The line was opened to the public on 24 August 1903 and was single throughout. The line had stations at North Connel (¾ mile), Benderloch (3 miles), Creagan (10 miles), Appin (13¼ miles), Duror (19 miles), Kentallen (22¾ miles), Ballachulish Ferry (25¾ miles) and Ballachulish (27¾ miles). Engineering works were heavy and included the Connel Ferry Bridge of 1,044ft over Loch Etive. The bridge was of the cantilever type with a single span of 500ft and was shared with the road from 1913. The Caledonian Railway ran a converted charabanc and trailer which it had built at St Rollox Works to convey passengers and cars from Connel Ferry to Benderloch in 1909. From 1913 the bridge was adapted to take cars but the road was closed when trains were crossing as there was not enough room for both. Gates were provided to prevent vehicular traffic crossing at the same time as the train. The railway also crossed Loch Creran at Creagan on a bridge with two lattice spans of 150ft placed on a central pier with castellated abutments.

The train service consisted of four trains each way on weekdays with an additional train on Saturdays under the BR regime with three of the trains going through to Oban. Trains connected at Ballachulish with the steamer for Kinlochleven before the road was built. Caley 0-4-4Ts of the '439' class worked the passenger trains with CR 0-6-0s on the freight. The line was closed to all traffic by BR on 28 March 1966, the freight service having been discontinued on 14 June 1965. The A828 road covers parts of the branch, notably Ballachulish to Ballachulish Ferry, Appin to Duror, Benderloch and the Connel Bridge. There is no trace of North Connel and little to see at Benderloch, Appin, Duror and Ballachulish Ferry. Creagan survives but is in a poor state but Kentallen is now part of a restaurant. At Ballachulish the building is now a medical centre with the car park over the old platform.

Caledonian 0-4-4T No 55224 leaves Oban with a smart three-coach set consisting of LNER Thompson coaches in 1960. The Caledonian '439' class lasted until 1962 under BR and a member (No 419) has survived and been restored by the Scottish Locomotive Preservation Society. *W. J. V. Anderson*

Oban was the terminus of the Caledonian line from Glasgow and some Ballachulish trains started from here. Caley tank No 55224 is seen in the terminus with the 4.55pm mixed on 8 June 1960. The engine was one of the McIntosh '439' standard passenger class 0-4-4Ts used for branch line and shunting work. *R. Hamilton*

Connel Ferry with Caley 0-4-4T No 55238 running round the 12.26pm Ballachulish to Oban on 8 June 1960. A fine lower quadrant and siding signal of pre-Grouping origin completes the scene. *R. Hamilton*

Caley 0-6-0 No 57587 plods away from Benderloch on the Ballachulish branch with a mixed freight consisting of stone and cement on 12 May 1962. The engine was one of the '812' class 0-6-0s built to the 1899 design of McIntosh, an example of which is preserved. *R. Hamilton*

The Connel Ferry bridge over Loch Etive carried both a road and a railway but when trains crossed, the road was closed. Standard Class 2 2-6-0 No 78052 is seen crossing with the 10.48am from Ballachulish to Connel Ferry on 2 May 1962. The road check-rail prevented vehicles from rubbing against the permanent way. *R. Hamilton*

The view from the train at North Connel shows the narrow wooden platform and the road access which was closed off when trains used the bridge. The notice warns motorists that the speed limit is 4mph and that vehicles are restricted to 6ft 6in in length. *Author*

Barcaldine Halt on the Ballachulish branch was a remote spot situated between Benderloch and Creagan. The halt had a siding for goods traffic and cattle pens on the platform. The platform shelter was lit by a single oil lamp which had a double vent and finial. *Lens of Sutton*

A general view of the Caledonian terminus at Ballachulish on 1 June 1957, with the CR signalbox and 0-4-4T waiting to depart. The branch was closed by BR in March 1966 and the station converted into a health centre with a car park over the platform site. *Author*

Inverness Branches

The ½-mile branch to Muirtown on the Caledonian Canal, approximately one mile from Inverness, was opened on 9 April 1877 and was goods only. A passenger service connection from the canal basin to Inverness was proposed but not implemented. The line was built without an Act which was later granted in 1890. The half-mile Inverness Harbour branch was opened on 6 November 1855, the same day as the Inverness & Nairn Railway. The canal basin was closed under BR on 1 January 1970 but the harbour branch sees some use with coal traffic.

Grampian

Alves to Hopeman (7½ miles)

The Inverness & Aberdeen Junction Railway opened its branch to Burghead on 22 December 1862, the Act having been passed on 17 May 1861. The branch was 5½ miles long and ran from Alves to Burghead Harbour. Coltfield Platform (opened as Wards) was built in 1864 and was situated 2¼ miles down the branch. The I&AJR became part of the Highland system in 1865. The extension to Hopeman was authorised on 4 July 1890 and the line opened on 10 October 1892. The new line left Burghead Harbour as a branch used by goods trains only as a new Burghead station was provided on the Hopeman section.

A station existed at Cummingston, half a mile short of Hopeman, but this was closed on 1 April 1904. Passenger services were withdrawn by the LMS on 14 September 1931 but freight ran until 30 December 1957 on the Hopeman section and 7 November 1966 to Burghead Harbour. The Highland Railway provided five trains per day on weekdays only. The Burghead Harbour branch was visited by the SLS/RCTS week-long tour of Scotland on 14 June 1960. The train was headed by ex-LMS '2P' 4-4-0 No 40663 but this was not the last passenger train as the 'Jones Goods', No 103, worked the line on 21 April 1962 on a SLS/BLS joint Easter tour. The trackbed from Burghead to Hopeman has been converted in recent years into a public footpath. Burghead station building remains but is in a poor condition while Hopeman is a caravan site reception centre.

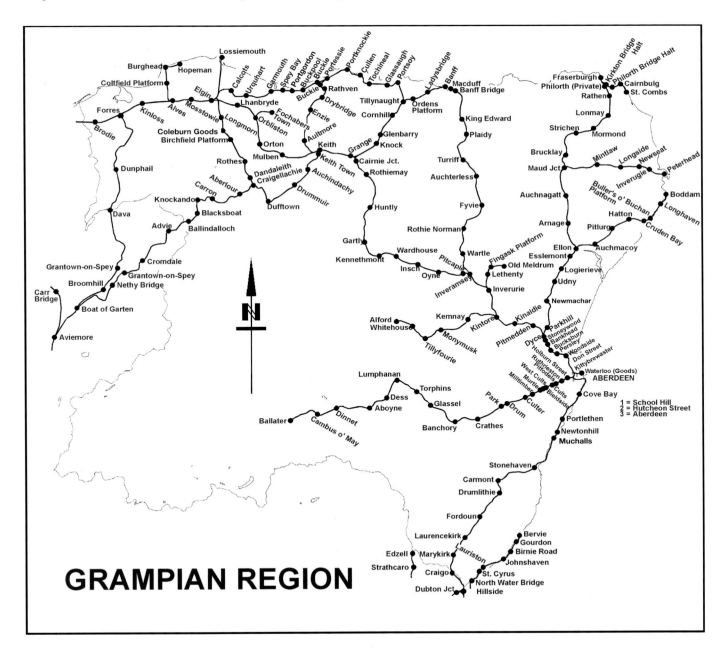

GRAMPIAN REGION

Early days at Hopeman showing vintage Highland coaches and 4-4-0 tank No 101 on a train of wooden-bodied stock with lower stepboards to enable boarding from rail level. No 101 was one of two locomotives purchased from Dubs in 1892 for the opening of the Hopeman extension. The engines were built for the Uruguay Eastern Railway which did not pay for them so Dubs sold them off. The 4-4-0Ts were known to locomen as 'Yankees' as they had a very South American appearance. *Commercial card*

Burghead sees the arrival of the SLS/RCTS week-long railtour on 14 June 1960. The passenger service was withdrawn by the LMS on 14 September 1931 but freight trains ran until 7 November 1966. No '2P' class 4-4-0s of LMS origin have survived into preservation. *Author*

'Jones Goods' No 103, the first 4-6-0 in Britain, charges uphill from Burghead Harbour with an SLS/BLS special on 21 April 1962. The branch closed to all traffic on 7 November 1966. *Author*

Kinloss to Findhorn (3 miles)

The Findhorn Railway was sanctioned by an Act of 19 April 1859 and opened on 18 April 1860. The Inverness & Aberdeen Junction Railway worked the line from 1 March 1862 but the railway ran at a loss and was closed on 1 January 1869 to passengers. The line was closed to all traffic c1873 and the rails removed, for the harbour at Findhorn had silted up. A relic that can be seen today is Station House, the former company offices.

Highland Railway No 103, resplendent in Stroudley yellow livery, arrives at Elgin on 21 April 1962 heading an Easter special from Inverness with a maroon set of BR Mk 1 coaches. The Elgin West stepboards were kept to enable passengers to alight from trains as the platforms were too low. *Author*

Lossiemouth station sees an LMS train on 2 May 1958 with '2P' class 4-4-0 No 40617 and LMS stock in BR maroon with yellow lining. The engine, built at Derby in 1929, did not last long after the photograph was taken as it was withdrawn in 1959. The passenger service survived until 6 April 1964. *Author*

Elgin to Lossiemouth (5½ miles)

The Lossiemouth branch of the former Great North of Scotland Railway was opened for traffic on 10 August 1852. The railway was promoted by the Morayshire Railway under an Act of 1846. The MR was absorbed into the GNSR on 1 October 1880 and the branch had a fairly healthy service of 12 trains per weekday under GNSR auspices. Under BR the service dropped to three trains per day on weekdays. The traffic declined as the station at Lossiemouth was some distance from the town centre where buses could whisk passengers off to Elgin in no time. The mainstay of the line was the fish traffic from the harbour to the south which was sent off in fitted freights. BR closed the line on 6 April 1964 to passengers and 28 March 1966 to freight. There is a footpath at Lossiemouth which is now in a park but little remains of the station.

Keith Junction to Elgin (27 miles)

The GNSR main line had reached Keith by 1856 and Dufftown by February 1862. The Speyside Railway continued on to Nethy Bridge (Abernethy) and was opened on 1 July 1863, the same day as the Morayshire Railway to Dandaleith. Both companies were later to become part of the GNSR system. The Morayshire Railway had opened the lines from Orton to Rothes and Dandaleith in 1858 and the 'main line' from Elgin to Rothes on 1 January 1862. The Morayshire

line from Orton to Rothes included a station at Sourden which was closed to passengers in 1866 and has since disappeared. The line saw the occasional goods to Rothes until 1886 but was lifted in 1907. The Morayshire was amalgamated into the GNSR in 1881. The Elgin to Keith line was closed to passengers on 6 May 1968, freight from Elgin to Craigellachie on 4 November 1968 and Craigellachie to Dufftown on 15 November 1971. Dufftown to Keith Junction has been retained pending preservation. The line had stations at Keith Town (½ mile), Auchindachy (3½ miles), Towiemore Halt (5 miles), Drummuir (6¼ miles), Dufftown (10¾ miles), Craigellachie (14½ miles), Dandaleith (15¼ miles), Rothes (17½ miles) and Longmorn (24 miles). The line was noted for the steep gradient and climb to Birchfield Summit between Elgin and Rothes on grades as steep as 1 in 50. At Keith Town no buildings survive but the K&DR plan to rebuild the station using the building from Kennethmont. Auchindachy station is now a private house, Towiemore has disappeared and Drummuir has been demolished. The track is still *in situ* from Keith to Dufftown and the station at Dufftown is being restored by the Keith & Dufftown Railway. There is no trace of the buildings at Craigellachie or Dandaleith. Rothes has been built over, Birchfield Halt has disappeared and there is no trace at Coleburn (closed in 1871 to passengers). Longmorn station buildings survive as part of an adjacent distillery.

Knockando station on the Speyside line in July 1959 sees the arrival of a Park Royal four-wheeled railbus. The station building in regional chocolate and cream colours dated from 1905 and was later used as a visitor centre for the distillery. *Author*

Craigellachie to Boat of Garten (33¼ miles)

The Strathspey line was authorised as the Strathspey Railway on 17 May 1861 from Dufftown to Abernethy via Craigellachie and opened on 1 July 1863. An extension to Boat of Garten was authorised on 5 July 1865 and opened on 1 August 1866 where a connection was made with the Highland Railway. Abernethy was renamed Nethy Bridge in 1867 and the two railways ran on separate tracks from Boat of Garten to the point of divergence south of Nethy Bridge. The Strathspey Railway was a satellite of the GNSR and was amalgamated into that concern in 1866. A connection was made at Craigellachie with the Morayshire Railway from Elgin upon opening in 1863, the Morayshire being absorbed into the GNSR at a later date. Stations and halts were provided at Aberlour (2¼ miles), Dailuaine (4¾ miles), Carron (5½ miles), Knockando (1905, 8 miles), Blacksboat (10¼ miles), Ballindalloch (12 miles), Advie (15¼ miles), Cromdale (21 miles), Grantown (24 miles) and Nethy Bridge (28½ miles). A private halt known as Knockando House Halt was opened in 1869, 1¼ miles from Carron. A station at Dalvey between Advie and Cromdale existed until 1868. The line was well known for the whisky distilleries which provided much traffic to the railway during its heyday.

Under BR the Scottish Region introduced lightweight diesel railbuses on 3 November 1958. In June 1959 BR opened some new rail-level halts. The new halts were at Imperial Cottages (6 miles), Gilbeys Cottages (7½ miles), Dalvey Farm (15½ miles) and Balliforth Farm (26½ miles). Tickets were issued by the guard who rode the railbus from Elgin to Aviemore, a distance of 51¼ miles. The BR railbuses ousted the steam working on passenger trains, the line being the last haunt of the GNSR 4-4-0s (LNER 'D40' class). The 'D40' class consisted of 21 engines, the design dating from 1899. The last member of the class, No 62277, survived in traffic until June 1958 and has since been restored in GNSR livery as No 49 *Gordon Highlander*. The economies effected by the use of the railbuses were short-lived as BR withdrew the passenger service on 18 October 1965. Boat of Garten to Aberlour freight traffic ceased from 4 November 1968 and Aberlour to Craigellachie on 15 November 1971. The trackbed today is a footpath from Craigellachie to Ballindalloch known as the Speyside Way. Craigellachie station site is now a car park, the building having been demolished. Aberlour station is now a tea rooms, Carron survives but is disused and Knockando was restored and served as a visitor centre for the distillery but is now out of use. Blacksboat survives with its goods shed and Ballindalloch is in use as a hostel. Advie has disappeared and Cromdale is a private residence, having been rebuilt. Grantown-on-Spey East survives but the building is disused whilst Nethy Bridge is a private residence for estate workers.

Above left:
Aberlour in July 1959 with a four-wheeled Park Royal railbus of 1958 unloading passengers by way of the platform steps. Mail is about to be loaded aboard in this truly vintage scene. *Author*

Left:
GNSR 4-4-0 No 49 double heads the SLS/RCTS 1962 special into Craigellachie with HR No 103 on 16 June 1962. The leading coaches are the two preserved Caledonian corridor coaches in the colours of that company. *R. Hamilton*

Above:
Grantown-on-Spey with Caledonian 0-6-0 No 57591 of the McIntosh '812' class heads a train of two ex-LMS coaches. The line was dieselised in 1959 with four-wheeled railbuses. *W. S. Sellar*

Orbliston Junction to Fochabers Town (3 miles)

The Inverness & Aberdeen Junction Railway was amalgamated with the Inverness & Nairn on 17 May 1861 having received the royal assent to build a line from Nairn to Keith on 21 July 1856. The line from Elgin opened on 18 August 1858 through to Keith enabling through working from Inverness to Aberdeen. The I&AJR became part of the Highland system on 29 June 1865. The Fochabers Town branch of the Highland was authorised on 1 July 1892 and opened on 16 October 1893, Orbliston Junction having been known as Fochabers until then. The railway terminated on the west bank of the River Spey about half a mile from the town. The GNSR station of the same name, Fochabers, was renamed Spey Bay in 1919. The Highland Railway provided six trains per weekday and an intermediate station at Balnacoul, ¾-mile from Orbliston Junction. The economy-minded LMS closed the branch to passengers on 14 September 1931 as traffic was light owing to the terminus being badly situated for the town. Freight lasted until BR days and was withdrawn on 28 March 1966. Nothing remains today of Balnacoul but the building at Fochabers is in use as a residential home.

The Fochabers Town branch of the former Highland Railway is seen being traversed by the 'Jones Goods' No 103 on 21 April 1962. The engine is propelling the special SLS/BLS train down the branch from Orbliston Junction and can be seen near the site of Balnacoul Halt. The LMS closed the line to passengers on 14 September 1931 and the Scottish Region to freight on 28 March 1966. *Author*

Enzie on the former Keith to Portessie branch is seen some time after closure which occurred during 1915. The line was opened in 1884 by the Highland in competition with the GNSR but was closed as a wartime economy. *Lens of Sutton*

HR No 103 leaves Aultmore on the former Keith to Portessie branch on 21 April 1962. The Keith to Aultmore section of the former Highland line was retained as a goods only line by the LMS and was not closed until 3 October 1966 under BR. *R. Hamilton*

GNSR 4-4-0 No 49 pauses at Huntly with the SLS/RCTS week's tour train on 14 June 1960. The tour visited most of the old GNSR branches that were still open for goods traffic at the time. The tour cost the then astronomical fare of £14 for the week. The locomotive is now in the Glasgow Transport Museum. *Author*

Keith to Portessie (13¾ miles)

The Highland built this line with the intention of gaining traffic from the coastal seaports and the farming district known as the Enzie. The Act was sanctioned on 12 July 1882 and the line opened on 1 August 1884. The Highland line ran parallel to the GNSR between Buckie and Portessie where the HR joined up and made use of the GNSR station. The railway was provided with three trains per weekday and had stations at Aultmore (2½ miles), Enzie (7¾ miles), Drybridge Platform (10 miles), Rathven (11¼ miles) and Buckie (12¼ miles). The line was closed on 9 August 1915 and the track removed. Aultmore to Keith remained for goods and survived into BR days, closing on 3 October 1966. The Buckie to Portessie section was closed to goods by the LMS on 1 April 1944. Little remains to be seen of the line today but Buckie station building survives.

Grange to Elgin (via Tillynaught) (39 miles)
Tillynaught to Banff (6 miles)

The Banff, Portsoy & Strathisla Railway received authorisation on 27 July 1857 and opened for traffic on 30 July 1859. The GNSR took over the railway in 1863 and worked it as part of their system. The GNSR and BP&SR were officially merged on 12 August 1867. Extension onwards to Elgin was authorised on 12 July 1882 and completed by 1 May 1886 to Elgin, Lossie Junction. The engineering works were heavy and included three viaducts at Cullen and a bridge over the River Spey near Garmouth. The spur at Cairnie was put in on 3 May 1886 and the station opened in 1898. The island platform station was unusual in that it was shown in the passenger timetable as an 'exchange platform only'. Stations were at Knock (8 miles from Keith Town), Glenbarry (9¼ miles), Cornhill (12¼ miles), Tillynaught (14½ miles), Portsoy (17¼ miles), Cullen (22¾ miles), Portknockie (24¾ miles), Findochty (26 miles), Portessie (27½ miles), Buckie (28¾ miles), Portgordon (31¼ miles), Spey Bay (33¾ miles), Garmouth (35 miles), Urquhart (38¼ miles) and Calcots (40¾ miles).

The Banff branch had stations and halts at Ordens Platform (1½ miles), Ladysbridge (3½ miles), Bridgefoot (4¾ miles), Golf Club House (5¼ miles) and Banff (6 miles). Banff station was at the harbour, had a single platform and an overall roof in timber. The original station, of a Victorian appearance, survived until closure. BR withdrew the passenger service of six trains per weekday on 6 July 1964 and the freight on 6 May 1968. Ladysbridge station building was removed after closure and used as a sports pavilion in Whitehills playing fields. On the coast line between Portsoy and Cullen,

Glassaugh station (2 miles from Portsoy) was closed on 21 September 1953. Further on, 2¼ miles from Glassaugh, Tochieneal station had been closed by BR on 1 October 1951. Buckpool, a mile beyond Buckie, was also closed by BR, from 7 March 1960. The Scottish Region introduced diesel traction to the line in 1961 and six trains per weekday were run, mostly from Aberdeen to Elgin. There was a summer Saturday train from Glasgow Buchanan Street to Elgin. BR withdrew the passenger trains and closed the line to all traffic from 6 May 1968. Parts of the old trackbed from Portknockie to Buckpool have been converted into footpaths as well as the Portsoy Harbour branch.

Today, Banff station site has been obliterated by a new road but at Ordens, which was one of the original stations of 1859, the platform and shelter survive. The station was closed originally in 1864 but reopened in 1917 as a halt, the halts at Bridgefoot and Golf Club House having opened in 1913. Ticket issuing machines were installed by the GNSR at these two halts — an early example of what today is considered to be a common sight. On the coast line nothing remains of Knock, Tillynaught, Cullen (now a housing estate), Portknockie, Findochty, Buckie, Portgordon, Garmouth or Calcots. Glenbarry is in a scrap yard, Cornhill is used by a coal merchant and Portsoy is now a scout hut with the old station converted for industrial use. At Glasshaugh and Tochieneal the platform edges survive whilst at Portessie some remains of the platforms can be seen. There is little trace of Buckpool. Spey Bay is now a house and Urquhart is used in a caravan park. The bridge over the Spey is used as a footpath and the viaducts at Cullen are listed structures.

Left:
Glassaugh station on the coast line, as seen in LNER days with GNSR 4-4-0 No 6826, later to become No 62261. The engine was built by Neilson & Co. in 1899 and classified 'D40' by the LNER (ex-GNSR 'V' class) and withdrawn by BR in February 1953. The train consists of pre-Grouping stock, the leading vehicle being ex-works in LNER brown. The station was closed on 21 September 1953 but the passenger service over the line lasted until 6 May 1968. *Lens of Sutton*

Above:
Tillynaught station with the branch train for Banff, with Class 2 2-6-0 No 78045 on 25 January 1964. The Banff branch only had a few months to go as the passenger service was withdrawn on 6 July 1964. Closure to all traffic took place with effect from 6 May 1968. *Author*

Below:
Ladysbridge was an intermediate station on the Banff branch which was opened by the Banff, Portsoy & Strathisla Railway on 30 July 1859, later to become part of the GNSR. Class 2 2-6-0 No 78054 is seen arriving on 21 April 1962 with a two-coach train of LNER stock. The station building was removed and resited as a sports pavilion after the closure of the line. *Author*

The terminus at Banff had an overall roof to protect passengers from the inclement weather and dated from pre-Grouping days. The line was opened originally in 1859 but was closed by BR on 6 July 1964. The site has since been covered by a new road. *Author*

GNSR six-wheeled coaches were a common sight around the system and many survived into BR days. A fine example is seen here at Glenbarry on 21 April 1962, having been turned into an engineers' mess van. Some vehicles were converted into camping coaches whilst others were sold off to farmers. *Author*

An aerial view of the GNSR terminus at Macduff on 13 June 1960 with the GNSR 4-4-0 No 49 on the SLS/RCTS tour. The layout shows the single platform with bay for fish vans, the goods shed, cattle dock and turntable with the two-road engine shed in the foreground. The passenger service was withdrawn by BR on 1 October 1950. *Author*

Inveramsay to Macduff (29¾ miles)

The line was sanctioned by Parliament on 15 June 1855 as the Banff, Macduff & Turriff Junction Railway. The line opened to Turriff on 5 September 1857, being worked from the start by the GNSR which provided three passenger trains per weekday. A further Act of 30 July 1866 authorised the extension to Macduff which was opened on 1 July 1871 as part of the GNSR system. The line was single throughout and all trains were mixed upon opening. Stations were built at Wartle (3¾ miles), Rothie Norman (7¼ miles), Fyvie (10¾ miles), Auchterless (14 miles), Turriff (18 miles), Plaidy (22½ miles), King Edward (24¾ miles), Banff Bridge (29½ miles) and Macduff (29¾ miles). The GNSR was running five trains per weekday prior to Grouping but BR closed the line to passengers on 1 October 1950. Freight traffic lasted until 1 August 1961 to Macduff and 3 January 1966 to Turriff. (Plaidy had been closed on 22 May 1944 under the LNER regime.) The terminus at Macduff was complete at closure, the GNSR signalbox, goods shed, turntable and cattledock being unaltered since the Grouping. The station building, in stone, accommodated a single track and had an overall roof.

The branch was visited in 1960 and 1962 by railtours and on both occasions the GNSR 4-4-0 No 49 *Gordon Highlander* worked the trains. The A97 road is now built over the old trackbed between Auchterless and Turriff for two miles. Wartle, Auchterless and Banff Bridge stations are now private residences and at Rothie Norman the platform edges have survived. At Fyvie the goods shed survives and at Turriff all buildings have been demolished as the road runs through the station site. The goods yard is a caravan site but the dock platform can be seen. Nothing remains of Plaidy (closed in 1944) but at King Edward the station buildings still exist. Macduff is now a Seaways net factory but the old engine shed survives.

Macduff station on 21 April 1962 is deserted as the regular freight traffic ceased to run on 1 August 1961 from Turriff. The signalling is still complete and has yet to be removed. The site is now occupied by a Seaways net factory but the engine shed has survived. *Author*

Banff Bridge station was a short distance from Macduff and consisted of a single platform with a wooden station building. The station was located near to Banff and was on the other side of the River Deveron from the town. The station is seen here on 21 April 1962 after the line was closed to all traffic. The building is now a private residence. *Author*

King Edward on the GNSR Macduff branch seen in April 1962 after the line had been closed by BR for nine months. The ornate station buildings have survived. *Author*

No 49 pulls away from Turriff on the GNSR Macduff branch on 21 April 1962. The passenger service was withdrawn on 1 October 1950 and freight north of Turriff on 1 August 1961. Freight traffic lasted to Turriff from Inveramsay until 3 January 1966. The A97 road runs through the station site. *Author*

Above:
No 49 *Gordon Highlander* is seen hard at work near Rothie Norman on the SLS/BLS Easter railtour of 1962. The scene looks natural as the organisers have not festooned the locomotive with unsightly headboards as is today's practice. Note the snow fence in the background. *Author*

Right:
GNSR No 49 has backed the Easter special into the platform at Old Meldrum for photographers on 21 April 1962. The engine is incorrectly restored in pre-1914 GNSR green and now resides in Glasgow Transport Museum. The line closed to passengers on 2 November 1931 and freight on 3 January 1966. The station site is now an industrial estate. *Author*

Old Meldrum with the branch goods in 1957 hauled by 'J72' class 0-6-0T No 68719, built at Darlington by the North Eastern in 1920 as a Worsdell 'E1' class. The LNER sent some 'J72s' to Scotland and No 68719 was the last engine in the class to have a wheel fastener on the smokebox door. The engine was withdrawn by BR in January 1961 and belonged to a class of locomotives built from 1898 to 1951. An example of the class, No 69023 built in 1951, has been preserved. *J. Britton*

Inverurie to Old Meldrum (5¾ miles)

The Inverurie & Old Meldrum Junction Railway was opened on 1 July 1856 under an 1855 Act and although independent, was worked by the GNSR from the start. The line left the GNSR main line 1¼ miles north of Inverurie station. Stations were provided at Lethenty (2¾ miles), Fingask Platform (3½ miles) and Old Meldrum, 5¾ miles from Inverurie. The GNSR provided five trains per weekday which terminated at Inverurie. Fingask was an unstaffed halt. The branch used motive power of a diminutive size and one of the Morayshire 2-2-2 tanks to the design of J. Samuel of 1859

was known to work the line. The GNSR built two steam railmotor units in 1905 for use on minor lines. One unit was tried out on the Old Meldrum and Alford branches as well as the Aberdeen suburban line but the units were not a success. In BR days ex-North Eastern Railway 'J72' class 0-6-0Ts were employed on the branch goods. BR withdrew the freight service on 3 January 1966, the LNER having withdrawn passenger trains on 2 November 1931. Today, nothing remains of Lethenty but the platform edge can be seen, Fingask has disappeared and the old station site at Old Meldrum is in commercial use.

Lethenty was one of the intermediate stations on the Old Meldrum branch closed to passengers on 2 November 1931. No 49 is seen passing the station which is in remarkably good condition in this 1962 scene. The building has since been removed but the platform edge remains. *Author*

Kintore to Alford (16 miles)

The branch opened for traffic on 21 March 1859, the Alford Valley Railway Act having been passed on 23 June 1856. The AVR was worked by the GNSR which had contributed towards the cost of construction. The GNSR later amalgamated with the AVR on 31 July 1866. The GNSR provided four passenger trains and a goods on weekdays only. Stations were located at Kemnay (4½ miles), Monymusk (7½ miles), Tillyfourie (10¾ miles), Whitehouse (13 miles) and Alford (16 miles). The GNSR signalling survived into BR days, the passenger service being withdrawn by the Scottish Region on 2 January 1950 and freight on 7 January 1966. Kemnay station has been built over, Monymusk demolished, Tillyfourie converted into a house and Whitehouse submerged in a scrap yard. Alford is now a transport museum complete with a narrow gauge railway.

The terminus at Alford in July 1961 shows the two-road engine shed and turntable of the former GNSR. The shed has been isolated from the track and used for storage following the passenger closure of 2 January 1950. Freight traffic was withdrawn on 3 January 1966. *J. R. Langford*

GNSR No 49 *Gordon Highlander* poses in the platform at Alford with the SLS/RCTS week's tour special on 13 June 1960. The two preserved Caledonian coaches are next to the engine with a GNSR starting signal overlooking the train. The line closed to all traffic on 3 January 1966. *Author*

Dyce to Peterhead (38 miles)
Maud Junction to Fraserburgh (16 miles)

The line was opened from Dyce to Peterhead on 3 July 1862 by the Formartine & Buchan Railway, a subsidiary of the GNSR, under an Act of 19 April 1859. A 1-mile-long branch from Peterhead station to the harbour followed on 9 August 1865. Through running from the joint station at Aberdeen took place on 4 November 1867. The Fraserburgh line from Maud was completed on 24 April 1865 under an Act of 21 July 1863. The Formartine & Buchan was merged into the GNSR on 1 August 1866. Stations were provided at Parkhill (1¼ miles), New Machar (5¼ miles), Udny (8¼ miles), Logierieve (10 miles), Esslemont (11½ miles), Ellon (13¼ miles), Arnage (16¾ miles), Auchnagatt (20½ miles), Maud Junction (24¾ miles), Mintlaw (28¾ miles), Longside (32 miles), Newseat Halt (34½ miles), Inverugie (35¾ miles) and Peterhead (38 miles). The GNSR provided four passenger trains per day to Peterhead and Fraserburgh on weekdays only.

On the Fraserburgh line stations and halts were sited at Brucklay (1¾ miles from Maud Junction), Strichen (5¾ miles), Mormond Halt (8¼ miles), Lonmay (10¾ miles), Rathen (13 miles), Philorth Halt (14½ miles) and Fraserburgh (16 miles). Philorth was private until 1924, Parkhill was closed on 3 April 1950 and Esslemont on 15 September 1952. The terminus at Peterhead had an island platform with an overall roof. The station had no run-round loop for the locomotive and trains, both goods and passenger, had to shunt by gravity. The harbour branch track fell into disuse and the track was lifted after World War 2. A 3-mile branch from Longside to a naval airship station at Lenabo was opened in 1915 and closed in 1920. The terminus at Fraserburgh consisted of three platforms and an overall roof which covered the carriage sidings. There was also a two-road engine shed. Granite, the local material, was in evidence in all the buildings, the station having been rebuilt in 1903 to accommodate the St Combs branch. BR provided a five-train service on both lines with the trains being split at Maud Junction. Passenger services were withdrawn to Peterhead on 3 May 1965 and Fraserburgh on 4 October 1965. The GNSR used its 4-4-0s on the passenger services, the 'D40' class surviving until the 1950s. BR introduced Standard Class 4 2-6-4 tanks and 'D34s' to replace these but steam gave way to diesel prior to closure and the rare but not very successful North British 'Type 2s' were employed. LNER 'B1s', 'B12s' and LMS '2Ps' were used on passenger and freight including the fish trains until usurped by more modern power. BR withdrew freight trains from Peterhead on 7 September 1970 and the last freight to Fraserburgh ran on 5 October 1979 hauled by Class 27 diesel No 27020. Most of the old trackbed from Dyce to Peterhead via Maud is now a footpath known as the Formartine & Buchan Way.

At Parkhill, the platform edge survives, New Machar is a house, Udny is a housing estate, Logierieve, Esslemont and Arnage are private houses and at Ellon the building survives but the rest of the site has been built over. Auchnagatt station site has been redeveloped and is now a housing estate. The buildings at Maud Junction, now a museum, are owned by the local authority and are complete with platforms. On the Peterhead branch, Mintlaw station was restored for local authority use but damaged by fire in 1997. At Longside there is a new house on the site of the station whilst Newseat and Inverugie stations are now private residences. Peterhead station site has been built over and is now a school and community centre. On the line to Fraserburgh, Brucklay, Rathen and Philorth are private houses and Strichen, Lonmay and Fraserburgh have been demolished. Fraserburgh is an industrial site but the old engine shed survives.

Below left:
Maud Junction with a North British 'Type 2' running round a two-coach train of ex-LMS stock in January 1964 prior to joining up the Peterhead and Fraserburgh portions for Aberdeen. The NBL 'Type 2' diesel-electric locomotives were not a great success and did not last for very long. *Author*

Above:
Peterhead was opened on 3 July 1862 by the Formartine & Buchan Railway, a subsidiary of the GNSR. The station had an island platform but no run-round loop so trains had to shunt by gravity. The line closed to passengers on 3 May 1965 and freight on 7 September 1970. A school and community centre have been built on the site. *Author*

Below:
Fraserburgh station in steam days with the St Combs branch train waiting in the branch platform headed by Class 2 2-6-0 No 46461. The fine stonework of the engine shed blends well with the other buildings in the town. *W. S. Sellar*

The Aberdeen train waits at Fraserburgh headed by a North British 'Type 2' diesel in January 1964. The line was closed to passengers on 4 October 1965 and freight on 5 October 1979. The site is now occupied by an industrial development but the engine shed survives. *Author*

Fraserburgh to St Combs (5 miles)

The Fraserburgh & St Combs Light Railway Order was passed on 8 September 1899 and the 5-mile light railway opened on 1 May 1903. The station at Fraserburgh was enlarged to accommodate the new line and was officially opened on 1 July 1903. The light railway started from Platform 3 and ran parallel to the main line for a mile before heading off for St Combs. Halts were provided at Kirkton Bridge (1 mile) and Philorth Bridge (2½ miles) and there was a station at Cairnbulg (3½ miles). The line had no signalling, a speed limit of 25mph and was worked as 'one engine in steam'. The GNSR used 'D' class 0-6-0Ts ('J90') which were followed by railmotors later to be withdrawn in 1906. The 1922 *Bradshaw* shows six trains per weekday with an extra on Saturdays. LNER 'J91s' were employed on the branch until 1926 when ex-NBR 4-4-0 tanks (Class D51) of Drummond design were employed. The 'D51' classes were replaced by ex-GER 'F4' class 2-4-2 tanks which in turn gave way to Ivatt or BR Class 2 2-6-0s. Steam power, which always worked with cow catchers, was superseded in 1959 by a twin-car Craven or Metro Cam diesel multiple-unit set which worked the line until closure which was effective from 3 May 1965 to all traffic. The branch was well patronised, the diesel service providing a service of ten trains per weekday with an extra on Saturdays. The problem was that the Fraserburgh to Aberdeen section was not so well used but the line was retained until 1979 for freight anyway! Parts of the line are now a public footpath. Little can be seen of the former stations and halts and St Combs station has been built over.

St Combs in steam days with Class 2 2-6-0 No 46461 on 9 August 1956. The branch was opened as a light railway on 1 May 1903 and worked by the GNSR. The branch was closed by BR on 3 May 1965 and the station site has now been built over. *W. S. Sellar*

St Combs had been reduced to basic station status by the time of closure. A two-coach Craven unit stands in the platform at St Combs on 25 January 1964. The line had been dieselised in 1959 but was closed to all traffic not long after this photograph was taken. *Author*

Ellon to Boddam (15½ miles)

The 15½-mile branch from Ellon to Boddam was opened by the GNSR on 2 August 1896 under an Act of 1893. The GNSR had ventured into the hotel business in Aberdeen including the Palace Hotel which had a covered way from the station platforms. A hotel and golf course were built at Cruden Bay and the line to Boddam was built to serve the new location. Stations on the Boddam branch were located at Auchmacoy (3¼ miles), Pitlurg (5½ miles), Hatton (8¼ miles), Cruden Bay (10¼ miles), Longhaven (13½ miles) and Boddam (15½ miles). A halt at Bullers o'Buchan was located between Cruden Bay and Longhaven. Four through trains to Boddam and two Cruden Bay workings were run by the GNSR prior to Grouping. The GNSR hotel at Cruden Bay was massive and was served by an electric tramway laid to 3ft 6½in gauge. The trams conveyed passengers and goods from the station to the hotel and the line was about half a mile long. There were two cars, both single-deck four-wheelers which were constructed at the company's works at Kittybrewster.

The hotel was not a financial success and the Boddam line closed to passenger traffic on 31 October 1932. The hotel was taken over by the Army during 1941 and after the end of the war was demolished. The tramway survived until 1940 and the cars were sold off for use as summer houses in nearby Hatton. BR closed the railway to all traffic on and from 31 December 1948. Following the railway's closure in 1932 the LNER provided a Rolls-Royce limousine from Aberdeen for hotel guests. The vehicle was numbered 2A 0004 in LNER stock with a registration number YR 4998. One wonders what sort of livery was used — perhaps the LNER coaching stock livery of varnished teak?

Today, Boddam has been built over and is a housing estate and Longhaven has disappeared as has Cruden Bay where the site is visible. Some foundations of the hotel can be seen, as can the old laundry building. The rest of the stations on the branch have been demolished but the goods shed at Hatton survives.

The Cruden Bay Hotel ran an electric tram from the station which was on the Boddam branch opened by the GNSR in 1896. The tram conveyed passengers and goods to the hotel on the 3ft 6½in gauge and survived until 1940. The two cars were built in the GNSR workshops and sold off by the LNER to be used as summer houses. *Lens of Sutton*

Aberdeen to Ballater (43¼ miles)

The Deeside Railway was authorised under Acts of 16 July 1846 and 28 May 1852 and opened for traffic on 8 September 1853. Trains ran from Ferryhill until 1854 when a terminus was opened at Guild Street. The line terminated at Banchory until it was extended to Aboyne on 3 December 1859 under the Aboyne Extension Act of 27 July 1857. The next stage in the line's future was the formation of the Aboyne & Braemar Railway and authorisation was granted on 5 July 1865 for an extension which was opened to Ballater on 17 October 1866. The line never got beyond Ballater but earthworks could be seen for a mile or so beyond the final terminus. The GNSR took over the Deeside and A&B Railways and from 31 January 1876 the branch became part of the Great North's system. A suburban service from Culter to Aberdeen was implemented in 1894 and new stations were opened. Seven of the line's suburban stations to Culter were closed by the LNER on 5 April 1937. The GNSR operated a bus connection from Ballater to Braemar from 2 May 1904 and this was taken over by the LNER in 1923 but railway ownership ceased in 1930 when the route was taken over by W. Alexander & Sons Ltd.

Under BR there were stations at Cults (3¾ miles), Culter (7½ miles), Park (10¾ miles), Crathes (14 miles), Banchory (17 miles), Glassel (21½ miles), Torphins (23¾ miles), Lumphanan (27 miles), Dess (29½ miles), Aboyne (32¼ miles), Dinnet (36¾ miles), Cambus o'May Halt (39½ miles) and Ballater (43¼ miles). Drum (9¾ miles) was closed on 10 September 1951 but a new halt at Dee Street (17½ miles) opened in 1961. The Deeside line was under Royal patronage right from the start and was used by Queen Victoria on her journeys to Balmoral. In addition to conveying the Royal Family, couriers' trains were run until 1938. The last Royal journey to Ballater took place on 15 October 1965 shortly before the branch was closed. Under BR the passenger service of six trains per weekday was approximately the same as that provided by the GNSR in 1922 but the timetable for that year does show an express service which stopped at Aboyne, Torphins and Banchory only. BR introduced multiple-unit railcars on the branch in the 1950s and from 1958 to 1962 used the unique battery-powered two-car unit. The use of this unit was short-lived and in appearance it looked like a diesel multiple-unit Derby lightweight car. The unit was numbered SC79998 and SC79999. BR closed the line to passenger traffic on and from 28 February 1966. Freight traffic was discontinued from Ballater to Culter on 18 July 1966 and Culter to Aberdeen

Aboyne on 1 May 1958 with Standard Class 4 2-6-4T No 80021 which has been fitted with a snowplough. The line was opened on 3 December 1859 and extended to Ballater on 17 October 1866. The station, since closure on 28 February 1966, has been converted into shop units. *Author*

(Ferryhill Junction) on 2 January 1967. Parts of the old trackbed have been turned into footpaths, notably Ferryhill to Culter (6¾ miles), Crathes to Banchory (3 miles), Dinnet to Ballater (4 miles) and Ballater towards Bridge of Gairn on the uncompleted Braemar extension. Ballater station is now council offices with a restaurant but in the tourist office opposite the GNSR Association has a museum which is well worth a visit.

Cambus o'May was reduced to halt status under BR and is now a summer cottage. Dinnet is an estate office and Aboyne has been converted into shop units. Dess is a pottery, Lumphanan, Torphins and Banchory have been built over but at Glassel the station house has survived. Crathes is still in situ as a residence and Park is used as offices in a caravan sales site. Drum has disappeared and Culter has been built over but the platform edge survives. Cults is used as a joiner's workshop and platform edges and buildings have survived at Pitfodels and Murtle (both closed in 1937) where the buildings are lived in.

Kittybrewster to Waterloo Goods (1¾ miles)
The 1 mile 53 chains from Kittybrewster to Waterloo Goods of the former GNSR was the original track of the main line until 1867 when the line to the joint station was opened. The line from Waterloo northwards had been authorised in 1854 and opened on 1 April 1856. The harbour was the haunt of the ex-GNSR 0-4-2 tanks classified 'Z4' and 'Z5' by the LNER and built by Manning, Wardle from 1915. The locomotives were withdrawn in 1960 but the Waterloo Goods branch is still in use to Croxton & Garry siding, the goods depot having been demolished and the yard sold off.

Aboyne on the Deeside line with battery-worked multiple-unit Nos SC79998 and SC79999 working a Ballater train on 1 May 1958. The battery unit was introduced in 1958 and lasted until 1962. The two-coach set resembled a Derby lightweight diesel and was designed at Derby and Cowlairs. One coach was the driving unit and the other the trailer, the traction motors being powered by 216 lead-acid cell batteries of 1,070A/hour capacity. *Author*

Tayside

Ballinluig was the junction for the former Highland Railway branch to Aberfeldy which, until 1961, was worked by Caledonian 0-4-4Ts of the '439' class. No 55217 has arrived in the branch bay on 31 August 1961 to connect with a Glasgow bound train. An example of the class, No 55189, has been preserved as CR No 419. *Author*

Ballinluig to Aberfeldy (8¾ miles)

The Highland branch to Aberfeldy opened to the public on 3 July 1865 under an Act of 1861. The single-track line had an intermediate station at Grandtully, 4¼ miles from Ballinluig. The LMS opened a halt at Balnaguard, 2¼ miles from Ballinluig on 2 December 1935 to serve an estate. The Highland Railway provided a service of six trains per weekday which was perpetuated through the LMS to the Scottish Region era. Mixed trains were run and through coaches were detached at Ballinluig for Perth and beyond on certain trains. The through coach service was in use by BR until the demise of the branch. The HR used its 2-4-0Ts, 4-4-0Ts and 0-6-4Ts. The LMS provided Caley 0-4-4Ts which worked the line until 1961 when they were replaced by BR Standard Class 4 2-6-4Ts. Dieselisation took place in 1962 and BR used 'Type 2s' in the 'D5100' and 'D5300' series until closure to all traffic on 3 May 1965. The old trackbed is now walkable, the station site at Aberfeldy being occupied by a housing estate. Little remains to be seen at Grandtully and a road now uses the old railway bridge over the River Tummel.

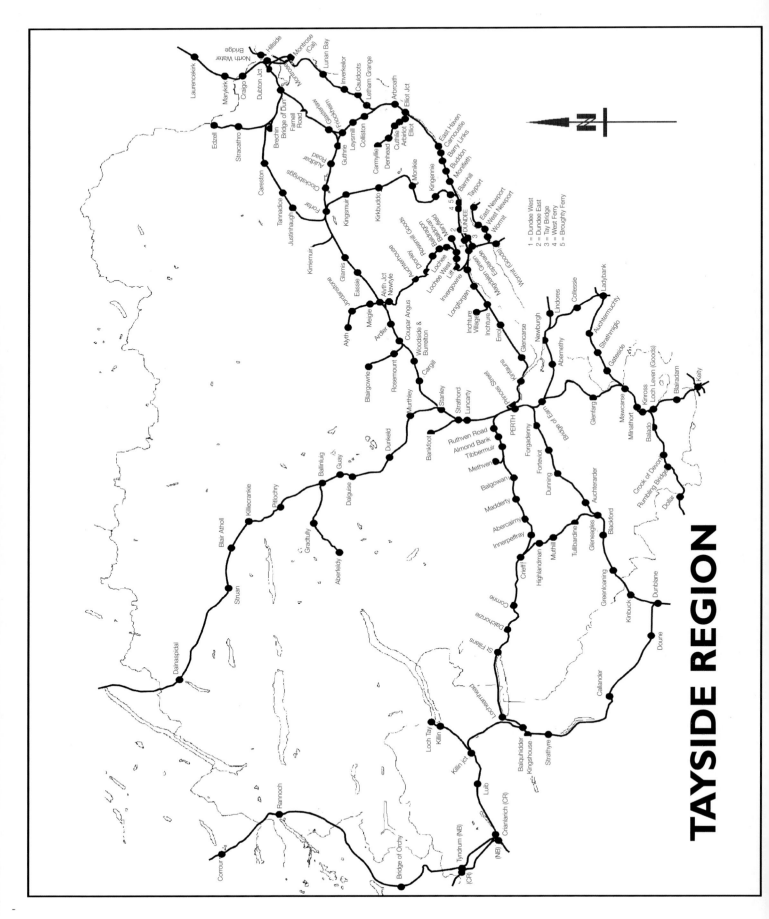

TAYSIDE REGION

1 = Dundee West
2 = Dundee East
3 = Tay Bridge
4 = West Ferry
5 = Broughty Ferry

The intermediate station on the Aberfeldy branch was at Grandtully which is depicted here in LMS days complete with publicity posters for the Highlands. *Lens of Sutton*

The branch terminus at Aberfeldy of the former Highland Railway with Caley 0-4-4T No 55217 and two ex-LMS coaches waiting to load up passengers on 31 August 1961. The 8¾-mile branch was closed by BR on 3 May 1965 and the site is now occupied by a housing development. *Author*

Strathord to Bankfoot (3 miles)

The Bankfoot branch left the Caley main line at Strathord, just over five miles from Perth, and was opened on 1 May 1906 as a light railway. The Bankfoot line had its own station at Strathord to which access was granted by means of a reverse shunt off the main line. The local company passed into the CR in 1913 and the LMS withdrew the passenger service on 13 April 1931, this having been killed off by a more direct bus route. BR withdrew the freight (seed potatoes) on 7 September 1964 and lifted the track shortly afterwards. The station existed within a caravan site but the branch has been mostly built over by the A9 road. The station site today has been covered by new housing.

Bankfoot shortly after opening in Edwardian days with a CR Drummond 0-4-4T and one coach waiting in the single platform. The line was opened on 1 May 1906 as a light railway but closed to passengers by the LMS on 13 April 1931. *Commercial card*

THE STATION, BANKFOOT. 661.

Above right:
Although Bankfoot was closed to passengers in 1931, it remained open until the BR era for freight trains. On 23 April 1962 the line was visited by a special organised by the BLS and SLS. Caledonian 0-6-0T No 56347 is seen arriving from Strathord with the loaded train to be greeted by the locals who are standing on the grass-grown platform. *Author*

Right:
Final days at Bankfoot on 20 April 1965 shortly after closure. The station was closed by the Scottish Region on 7 September 1964 to all traffic and later utilised in a caravan site but recently a housing development has occupied the site. *E. Wilmshurst*

Branch line motive power was provided by the Caledonian which built 24 0-4-4Ts from 1884 to 1891 to the design of D. Drummond. No 15103, formerly No 1177, was built in 1886 but did not survive into BR ownership as the class had all been withdrawn by 1944 under the LMS.
Lens of Sutton

Coupar Angus to Blairgowrie (4¾ miles)

The Caley branch to Blairgowrie was opened on 1 August 1855 by the Scottish Midland Junction Railway under an Act of 1853 and had a through train service to Dundee. The service of five trains per weekday was supplemented by five Coupar Angus to Blairgowrie workings just prior to the Grouping. The through service to Dundee ran via the Dundee & Newtyle Railway, an extension of the D&NR in the form of the Newtyle & Coupar Angus Railway having been opened for traffic in 1837. The Scottish Midland Junction Railway opened from Perth to Forfar on 2 August 1848 and replaced the D&NR sections between Coupar Angus, Newtyle and Glamis.

On the Blairgowrie branch there was an intermediate station at Rosemount, 1½ miles from Blairgowrie. Blairgowrie station had a fine overall roof covering a single platform and a goods shed. There was also an engine shed dating from Caledonian days. The passenger service was withdrawn by the Scottish Region on 10 January 1955. Freight traffic was terminated by BR from 6 December 1965. Most of the branch is now a footpath but parts of the trackbed have been sold off. The station site at Blairgowrie is now an industrial estate with the old engine shed reconstructed for use by the county council. Rosemount station is now a private house and the old trackbed is walkable most of the way through to Coupar Angus.

Below left:
Blairgowrie on 23 April 1962 with the BLS/SLS railtour and Pickersgill Caledonian 4-4-0 No 54465. The engine was built at St Rollox as CR No 121 in February 1916 and lasted until October 1962 under BR. The class was extinct by December 1962 and regrettably no examples of the class survived. In the background the combined station and goods shed can be discerned. Passenger services were withdrawn on 10 January 1955 and freight on 6 December 1965. *Author*

Below:
Alyth Junction was on the now defunct Caledonian main line from Perth to Kinnaber Junction. Caley 0-6-0 No 57441 heads the SLS/RCTS special on 16 June 1960 with the two preserved CR coaches leading the train. The 'Jumbos' were of a large class of 244 engines built from 1883 to 1897. No 57441 was built by the CR at St Rollox in 1896 to the design of Dugald Drummond. The class survived until the BR era and was extinct by 1963. *Author*

Meigle station on the Alyth branch seen from the window of a BR Mk 1 coach on 23 April 1962. The passenger service was withdrawn in 1951 and goods in 1965 but the station is still in good condition in this 1962 view. *Author*

A view of Jordanstone on the Alyth branch in LMS days shows the station building to be in good condition and the Caledonian nameboard to be still in situ. A loaded wagon has been dropped in the goods loop where it will probably be unloaded. *Lens of Sutton*

Alyth to Alyth Junction (5¼ miles)

The Alyth Railway opened for business on 2 September 1861 and was leased to the Scottish North Eastern Railway in 1864 which became part of the Caledonian system in 1866. (The Alyth Railway was absorbed by the Caledonian in 1875.) Intermediate stations were at Meigle (1¼ miles) and Jordanstone (3¼ miles). Alyth Junction was known as Meigle until 1876 when Fullarton was renamed Meigle. The Alyth Junction to Newtyle section opened in 1868 to connect with the rebuilt Dundee & Newtyle Railway. Under the Caledonian the service on the branch consisted of seven trains per weekday with extras run on Saturdays. The CR opened a stopping point entitled Pitcrocknie Platform which was one mile from Alyth and renamed Pitcrocknie Siding by the LMS. The LMS reduced the service drastically prior to Nationalisation and the Summer 1947 timetable shows only two trains from Alyth, one at 6.40am and one at 5.50pm. A passenger service of this nature could not generate much business but this traffic continued until 2 July 1951 under the Scottish Region. Freight traffic lasted longer and finally ceased in 1965, the official closure date being 1 March 1965. Alyth station site is now a housing estate and Meigle is a contractor's yard. At Jordanstone the station house survives.

Two views of Alyth which was opened on 2 September 1861 by the Alyth Railway, later to become part of the Caledonian system. The original station had an overall roof which was later removed. The passenger service lasted until 2 July 1951 and freight until 1 March 1965. The station site has been built over and is now a housing estate. *Lens of Sutton/Author*

Alyth Junction to Dundee West (18 miles)

This section of line ran over the former Dundee & Newtyle Railway which was extensively rebuilt during the period 1860-1868. There were stations at Newtyle (1¼ miles), Auchterhouse (5½ miles), Dronley (7 miles), Baldragon (9¼ miles), Baldovan & Dronfield (10¼ miles), Lochee (12 miles), Lochee West (12¾ miles) and Liff (13¾ miles). The railway was one of the earliest in Scotland and was authorised on 26 May 1826 from Dundee to Newtyle (old). The line included three cable-worked inclines of 1 in 10, 1 in 13 and 1 in 25. Another Act was passed on 29 May 1830 to drum up more money and trains commenced on 16 December 1831. Steam power was introduced in 1833 to work on the 4ft 6½ in gauge line which was converted to standard gauge in 1849. The terminus was in Ward Road, Dundee where trains ascended the 1 in 10 Law Hill incline. A line continued from Ward Road down to the docks and was in use until 1861. The line was worked by the Dundee, Perth & Aberdeen Junction Railway in 1848, the Scottish Central Railway in 1863 and the Caledonian in 1865. Improvements to iron out the inclines were implemented in 1860, 1861 and 1868 when the connection to the main line at Alyth was put in from Newtyle. Lochee West was closed as a wartime economy on 1 January 1917 and the D&NR was officially merged into the LMS in 1923. At Grouping there were six trains per weekday with two extras on Saturdays. BR withdrew the passenger service on 10 January 1955 and the section from Newtyle Junction to Auchterhouse on 5 May 1958 to freight. The section from Auchterhouse to Fairmuir Junction closed to freight on 25 January 1965 and Maryfield Goods to Ninewells Junction on 6 November 1967. The Newtyle Goods to Alyth Junction part closed to all traffic on 7 September 1964. Dundee West closed to passengers on 3 May 1965. Parts of the line are now footpaths or parkland including the Maryfield Goods branch. Newtyle old station is now in use as a container store and Crossroads station building survives in King's Cross Hospital grounds as a dwelling house. A platform survives at Baldragon and Lochee is now the Lochee Burns Club but little remains of the other stations.

Dronley on the Dundee to Newtyle branch with the pick-up goods hauled by CR 0-6-0 No 55786 of the McIntosh '812' class of 1899, an example of which has been preserved. Bridgefoot to Dronley is now a footpath. *W. S. Sellar*

Lochee West was on the Dundee to Newtyle line of the former Caledonian Railway and closed to passengers in 1917. The station was retained for goods and parcels after the passenger closure and had an unusual design in the roof with ornate clover leaf ironwork brackets supporting the canopy. *Lens of Sutton*

Kirriemuir terminus on 16 June 1960 with 'Jumbo' Class 2F No 57441 with the SLS/RCTS railtour special. The line was opened in 1854 and closed by the Scottish Region on 4 August 1952. Freight traffic lasted until 21 June 1965 and the station was subsequently demolished. *Author*

Kirriemuir Junction to Kirriemuir (3¼ miles)
A branch of the Scottish Midland Junction Railway, the line was opened in November 1854 under an Act of 1853. A junction station existed from 1858 until 1864, thereafter trains for Kirriemuir ran from Forfar. The Caledonian ran nine passenger trains per weekday with an extra on Tuesdays, Fridays and Saturdays over the branch from Forfar before World War 1 and 11 prior to the Grouping. The LMS perpetuated a similar service but reduced it to three each way during World War 2. BR withdrew passenger trains on 4 August 1952 while freight traffic lasted until 21 June 1965. Kirriemuir station site has been cleared.

Forfar and Broughty Ferry (17¾ miles)
The former Caledonian line from Forfar to Broughty Ferry was opened to passenger traffic on 14 November 1870.

Intermediate stations were built at Kingsmuir (2¾ miles), Kirkbuddo (5¾ miles), Monikie (9¾ miles), Gagie (13 miles), Kingennie (14¼ miles) and Barnhill (16½ miles). The CR provided a train service from Dundee East to Barnhill of 11 trains per weekday with four going through to Forfar and Kirriemuir with an extra market train which Tuesdays and Fridays. The passenger service was continued by the LMS on a similar pattern, the last section from Broughty Ferry Junction to Dundee East being over the Dundee & Arbroath Joint line. BR withdrew the passenger service on 10 January 1955, the freight from Forfar to Kingsmuir on 8 December 1958 and Kingsmuir to Broughty Ferry Junction on 9 October 1967. Dundee East to Camperdown Junction closed to passengers on 5 January 1959. The halt at Gagie had been opened by the LMS during the 1930s.

Dundee East, seen on 8 October 1958, was the terminus of the Dundee & Arbroath Joint line and was closed on 5 January 1959. The ex-NBR 'C16' class 4-4-2T is shunting empty stock out of the 1857 terminus. *W. S. Sellar*

Forfar to Brechin (15¼ miles)

The Forfar & Brechin Railway (worked by the Caledonian) opened to Brechin for passengers on 1 June 1895 where the terminus was a dead-end served by trains from Edzell (opened in 1896) and Bridge of Dun. The CR provided four passenger trains per weekday with an extra on market days. Intermediate stations were built at Justinhaugh (4¾ miles), Tannadice (6½ miles) and Careston (10¼ miles). By 1923 when the line became part of the LMS system, there were five trains per weekday. The LMS reduced the service to two trains prior to 1948 and BR withdrew the passenger service on 4 August 1952. Freights were withdrawn from Brechin to Careston on 7 March 1958 and Careston to Justinhaugh on 7 September 1964. The final piece to Forfar was closed to all traffic on 4 September 1967. Tannadice is now a house, Justinhaugh has been incorporated into a tractor repair works and Careston now has a house on the station site.

Guthrie to Arbroath (7¾ miles)

The Arbroath & Forfar Railway was promoted as early as 1835 and was unusual in that the gauge was 5ft 6in. An Act was passed on 19 May 1836 and the first section of this railway opened for business on 24 November 1838. The passenger services were worked by horses, the first section being from Arbroath to Leysmill. The section to Forfar (Playfield) was opened on 4 December 1838 but steam traction was not introduced until 3 January 1839. The gauge was converted to standard from 1846 to 1848 and the Aberdeen Railway took over the line on 1 February 1848

when the future main line was opened from Guthrie through Glasterlaw to Montrose. The Aberdeen Railway and Scottish Midland Junction became the Scottish North Eastern in 1856, to be merged into the Caledonian on 10 August 1866. The section of track from Glasterlaw to Friockheim was closed on 1 February 1908 and was lifted in 1917. Guthrie to Arbroath (St Vigean's Junction) became a minor line with 11 passenger trains per weekday connecting out of the Caley main line at Guthrie. From Guthrie passenger stations were located at Friockheim (1¼ miles), Leysmill (2¾ miles) and Colliston (4¼ miles). The passenger service was withdrawn on 5 December 1955 and the freight cut back to Colliston (from St Vigean's) on 1 January 1959. The final part from Colliston to Guthrie was closed to freight on 25 January 1965. A strange twist of fate saw the former Caledonian main line from Stanley Junction to Kinnaber Junction closed to passengers on 4 September 1967, the part from Forfar to Bridge of Dun being closed to all traffic. The Arbroath Harbour branch was used until 1 November 1963 and the original terminus at Forfar Playfield used as a coal depot until 31 October 1979. Freight survived on the old main line from Stanley Junction to Forfar until 1982. The last train run was a railtour organised by the Angus Railway Group on 5 June 1982 hauled by 'Type 4' No 40143.

Friockheim and Leysmill are private residences but Colliston has disappeared. A footpath commences along the old trackbed at Colliston for Arbroath and the impressive gateway under the old railway formation survives at Guthrie.

Left:
The end of the line at Careston in April 1962 when the station was still complete although passenger services were withdrawn on 4 August 1952. The section of the line from Brechin to Careston was closed completely on 7 March 1958 and Careston to Justinhaugh on 7 September 1964. *Author*

Right:
The Guthrie Gate has outlasted the railway which it once carried. The Caledonian Railway inherited the line from the Arbroath & Forfar Railway which was obliged to build the gate by the occupants of Guthrie Castle. The Guthrie Gate was built in mock Tudor with turrets, battlements, shields and a coat of arms. *Author*

Stracathro on the Edzell branch with ex-NBR 'B' class (LNER Class J37) No 64587 on the goods. The Edzell branch was opened by the Caledonian on 1 June 1896 but closed to passengers by the LMS on 27 April 1931 which reinstated it in 1938 and finally withdrew it on 27 September of that year. The station is now a private residence. *W. S. Sellar*

The lengthy platform at Edzell has become disused in this 1962 view taken on the occasion of a visit by the 'Scottish Rambler' railtour. The passenger service was withdrawn in 1938 but goods traffic lingered on until 7 September 1964. The site is now occupied by a housing development. *Author*

The Brechin station exterior today has been restored and now boasts a Caledonian Railway name which has replaced the LMS ironwork. The railway runs a regular service to Bridge of Dun on the former main line. *Author*

Brechin to Edzell (6½ miles)

The Edzell branch opened to passengers on 1 June 1896 and was worked by the Caledonian Railway. An intermediate station was provided at Stracathro (renamed from Inchbare in 1912) at Milepost 4½. A weekday service of five trains was provided with an extra on Saturdays. By the Grouping the service had increased to eight trains but the impoverished LMS withdrew the passenger service on 27 April 1931. The service was restored for a brief period during the summer of 1938 but suspended again on 27 September 1938. BR withdrew the freight on and from 7 September 1964 and the branch was visited by the 'Scottish Rambler' railtour on 22 April 1962. Edzell station site is now a housing estate and Stracathro station building is now a private residence.

The exterior of the Caledonian terminus at Brechin on 22 April 1962 with the LMS sign still in position on the canopy 14 years after Nationalisation. The building was in a very good condition at the time considering that the passenger services were withdrawn on 4 August 1952. *Author*

Bridge of Dun to Brechin (4 miles)

Brechin was first reached by the Aberdeen Railway in 1848 when a directors' special arrived on 27 January from Montrose and Guthrie which was originally on the Arbroath & Forfar Railway. The Aberdeen Railway, authorised in 1845, became part of the Caledonian system by the process of amalgamation. A fairly frequent service of 14 passenger trains per weekday was provided. The dead-end terminus at Brechin eventually saw a service for three lines during the heyday of the CR. The Brechin avoiding line (opened in 1895) was lifted in 1917 and not reinstated. BR withdrew the passenger service on 4 August 1952 but freight survived until 4 May 1981. The Brechin Railway Preservation Society, now the Caledonian Railway (Brechin), occupies the Brechin to Bridge of Dun section where both stations have been restored. The Brechin station frontage now displays the Caledonian Railway name in the ironwork.

Above:
Brechin station was a terminus and was served by three lines, Bridge of Dun, Edzell and Forfar trains all terminating here in the heyday of the Caledonian Railway. The Edzell branch goods is being shunted by 'J37' No 64587 on 1 March 1961 in what is now the Caledonian Railway's terminus. The engine, built in 1918 by the North British Locomotive Co, lasted until June 1964 under BR. *W. S. Sellar*

Below:
Ivatt Class 2 2-6-0s Nos 46463 and 46464 pose at Montrose NBR station prior to taking the train to Elliot Junction for the Carmyllie branch with the Easter 1962 'Scottish Rambler'. The train has just traversed the Inverbervie branch and the second engine, No 46464, was later to be preserved. *Author*

Below Right:
North Water Bridge viaduct on the ex-NBR Inverbervie branch is now a listed structure. The 'J37' 0-6-0, No 64615 built by NBL in 1920, struggles up the incline in this 1960 view with the SLS/RCTS railtour. *Author*

Dubton to Montrose (3 miles)

The Aberdeen Railway reached Montrose on 1 February 1848 with a line from Friockheim and Guthrie. The line was built under an Act of 1845 and became a branch of the main line when it was extended from Dubton to Stonehaven on 1 November 1849. The AR eventually opened to Aberdeen (Ferryhill) in 1850 on what was to become the CR main line. The North British did not arrive on the scene until 1880 to create the well known competition between the rival companies with the junction at Kinnaber. The Caley Montrose branch had 14 passenger trains per weekday in 1923 but the LMS rationalised the service from 30 April 1934 when LMS trains were diverted to the former NBR station via Broomfield Junction. BR withdrew the passenger trains from Dubton to Montrose NBR on 4 August 1952. The CR main line passenger service from Perth to Kinnaber Junction was withdrawn on 4 September 1967. Dubton and Broomfield Junction was closed to all traffic from 23 June 1963 and the Montrose Caley branch on 19 June 1967.

Montrose to Inverbervie (13 miles)

The Aberdeen Railway opened the main line throughout in 1850. The AR amalgamated with the Scottish Midland Junction in 1856 to become the Scottish North Eastern which later became part of the Caledonian. Montrose Caledonian had opened on 1 February 1848 as a part of the Aberdeen Railway and as a result became a branch off the main line from Dubton, a distance of three miles. An independent railway, the Montrose & Bervie Railway was promoted and authorised on 3 July 1860. The M&BR opened on

1 November 1865 and was worked by the SNER. The NBR took over the M&BR on 1 October 1881, not having arrived on the scene until August when the NBR Arbroath to Kinnaber Junction section was opened. Montrose CR station closed to passengers on 29 April 1934 when all trains ran to the NBR station. The old CR station at Montrose lasted until BR days and closed to goods on 19 June 1967 to Broomfield Junction, the part through to Dubton having closed from 23 June 1963 to all traffic.

The Inverbervie branch had stations at North Water Bridge (3¼ miles), St Cyrus (5¼ miles), Lauriston (6¼ miles), Johnshaven (8½ miles), Birnie Road Siding (10 miles), Gourdon (12 miles) and Inverbervie (13 miles). Three weekday trains were run with an extra on Saturdays. The passenger service was withdrawn on 1 October 1951 and the freight on 23 May 1966. Bervie was renamed Inverbervie in 1926 and had a single platform and a goods yard. North Water Bridge and Birnie Road Siding were halts, the latter being served on Fridays only for Montrose market. The SLS/RCTS special week's tour of Scotland visited the line on 16 June 1960 worked by Reid NBR 0-6-0 No 64615 of the LNER 'J37' class. The line was visited on 22 April 1962 by an SLS/BLS railtour but this time the motive power was a 'Type 1' EE diesel, No D8028. A last train ran on 22 June 1966 utilising 'J37' class 0-6-0 No 64547. Inverbervie is now a car park, Gourdon station house survives, Johnshaven is now a housing estate, at Lauriston there is little to see, St Cyrus has been demolished and Montrose (CR) is now a nursing home. The viaduct over the River North Esk survives and is a listed structure.

The terminus at Inverbervie on the occasion of the BLS/SLS Easter railtour visit in 1962. The station opened as Bervie on 1 November 1865 and was renamed by the LNER in 1926. The passenger service was withdrawn on 1 October 1951. *Author*

The spruced up 'J37' class 0-6-0 is seen at the terminus at Inverbervie on 16 June 1960 with the SLS/RCTS week's railtour. The train is a real hotchpotch of stock and includes the two Caley coaches as well as a GER buffet car. The engine survived until 1963 and the branch until 1966. The platform survives on a bird-watching site. *Author*

The Montrose Caledonian Railway station was closed to passengers on 29 April 1934 and the Inverbervie trains diverted to the North British station. The single-platformed station is seen here after closure with pre-Grouping stock in store. The line closed to goods traffic on 19 June 1967 and the station site is now a nursing home. *Lens of Sutton*

Elliot Junction with Ivatt 2-6-0s Nos 46463 and 46464 bringing the 'Scottish Rambler' into the platform having worked the train from Carmyllie, the terminus of the Carmyllie Light Railway, part of the former Dundee & Arbroath Joint Railway. *Author*

Ivatt Class 2s Nos 46463 and 46464, built at Crewe in 1950, leave Elliot Junction on the climb to Carmyllie. Passenger services commenced on this 5-mile line on 1 February 1900 and ceased on 2 November 1929. Freight lasted on the branch until 24 May 1965. *Author*

Elliot Junction to Carmyllie (5 miles)

The Carmyllie Light Railway was part of the Dundee & Arbroath Joint Railway (NBR and CR). The line started as a private mineral railway in 1854 and was not opened to passengers until 1 February 1900 as a light railway. Passenger stations were provided at Arbirlot (1¼ miles), Cuthlie (2 miles), Denhead (3½ miles) and Carmyllie (5 miles). Stations were built economically to say the least as the terminus at Carmyllie was of one-coach length only. The 1922 *Bradshaw* shows two trains only, both through to Arbroath — one in the morning and one in the afternoon with corresponding return workings. The railway was very much a twister and bender as far as the alignment was concerned and had a gradient as steep as 1 in 36 on the climb to Carmyllie which was 600ft above sea level. The passenger service ceased from 2 November 1929 but freight survived until 24 May 1965 under BR. Nowadays a footpath runs from Elliot Junction to Arbirlot. There is not much to see otherwise as light railways tend to be built on the cheap. The Carmyllie Light, authorised on 6 August 1898, was the first light railway in Scotland to be built under the 1896 Act.

Carmyllie station on the branch from Elliot Junction was one of the smallest stations in Britain, if not the smallest. The platform could just accommodate a single coach. Photograph taken on 16 June 1960. *Author*

Inchture to Inchture Village (2 miles)

The main line of the Dundee & Perth Railway opened for traffic on 24 May 1847 with the terminus at Perth on the east side of the River Tay at Barnhill. When the railway was proposed Lord Kinnaird objected to the line coming close to his residence at Rossie Priory so the railway missed Inchture by two miles. A branch was opened from the main line station to the village in 1848 and was worked by horse. The passengers were conveyed in 'dandies' (coaches on rails) and accommodation consisted of two classes. A similar 'train' worked the North British Port Carlisle branch and has been preserved. The Inchture Village horse tram worked until it was withdrawn from 1 January 1917 as a wartime economy. A similar line existed at Errol from 1849 to 1852. The old tram terminus, stables and workers' dwellings survive at Inchture Village as residences.

Inchture Village was served by a horse-worked tram owned by the Caledonian Railway, a unique arrangement. The Edwardian scene taken from a commercial card depicts the terminus and tramshed. Today, the shed, stables and railwaymen's houses remain although turned into private dwellings. *Commercial card/Author's collection*

The Methven branch was opened by the Almond Valley & Methven Railway on 1 January 1858 and closed by the LMS on 27 September 1937. NBR No 256 *Glen Douglas* leaves Methven Junction on 23 April 1962 with the 'Scottish Rambler'. No 256 was built at Cowlairs in 1913 and restored to NBR livery in 1959. *Author*

Methven station in LMS days shows the single-road engine shed and basic station building with the timetable posted inside the waiting room. The site is now an industrial estate. *Lens of Sutton*

Methven with the SLS/RCTS Scottish railtour on 15 June 1960 and the Pickersgill 4-4-0 No 54485 at the head of the train, having run round the five-coach formation. The engine was built at St Rollox in September 1920 and withdrawn at Perth in October 1961. *R. Hamilton*

Perth to Balquhidder (39 miles)
Methven Junction to Methven (1 mile)

The Almond Valley Junction to Methven line was opened by the Perth, Almond Valley & Methven Railway on 1 January 1858 under an Act of 1856. Extension from Methven Junction to Crieff followed on 21 May 1866 with the Crieff & Methven Junction Railway authorised in 1864. Crieff to Comrie followed on 1 June 1893, having been authorised in 1890 and the final section on to Balquhidder along the side of Loch Earn reached the Caledonian Oban line on 1 May 1905. The engineering works on the final section were costly and included the Lochearnhead viaduct as the CR intended to develop tourist traffic over this scenic route. Stations and halts were built at Ruthven Road (3 miles from Perth), Almondbank (4 miles), Tibbermuir (5 miles), Balgowan (9 miles), Madderty (11½ miles), Abercairny (13½ miles), Innerpeffray (15¾ miles), Crieff (17¾ miles), Comrie (23¾ miles), St Fillans (29½ miles) and Lochearnhead (37 miles). A request stop was provided at Dalchonzie Platform (26½ miles).

The passenger service was from Perth to Crieff with the occasional working through to Balquhidder and a connecting train from Methven. The passenger service was more or less the same throughout the line's history. The Balquhidder to Comrie section was closed to all traffic on 1 October 1951, the same day that the passenger service from Crieff to Perth (Almond Valley Junction) was discontinued. The Methven passenger service was withdrawn by the LMS on 27 September 1937 but freight continued on the mini branch until 25 January 1965. Comrie to Crieff closed to all traffic on 6 July 1964 and Crieff to Almond Valley Junction on 11 September 1967. Most of the old trackbed is now walkable right the way through to Lochearnhead. Methven station is now an industrial estate, Almondbank, Abercairny and Innerpeffray are now houses, Comrie has been demolished, St Fillans station building and signalbox are in a caravan site and Lochearnhead is now a scout hostel. The viaduct at Lochearnhead still stands and Dalchonzie signalbox has survived. Madderty is now a house and Balgowan has been built over but the old crossing house has survived.

Above:
Restored 'Glen' class No 256 passes Balgowan on the Perth to Crieff line with the 'Scottish Rambler' on 23 April 1962. The meagre passenger building and goods shed have survived in this 1962 scene where passenger services were withdrawn on 1 October 1951. *Author*

Above right:
Madderty on the Perth to Crieff line where the June 1960 special stops for photographs while local residents look on. This section of the former Caledonian Railway was opened on 21 May 1866 under an 1864 Act. The station is now a private house. *Author*

Right:
Abercairny with the 1960 week-long railtour organised by the SLS and RCTS shows the unusual layout with a short passenger platform and the lengthy cattle dock crammed full of old vans. The station is now a private residence. *Author*

Above:
A study of Innerpeffray in LMS days with the old Caledonian nameboard still in position. Other CR features are the oil lamps and the station clock. The line was closed to passengers on 1 October 1951. The station building is now a house. *Lens of Sutton*

Below:
The Pickersgill 4-4-0 No 54485 stops briefly for photographers in this truly Caledonian scene on 15 June 1960 at Innerpeffray. The engine lasted only a few months later and was withdrawn in October 1961. *Author*

Above right:
No 54485 has brought the special into Crieff station on 15 June 1960. The substantial two-platform station with lengthy platforms and cast iron overbridge has now been built over and is a medical centre with an ambulance station. *Author*

Gleneagles to Crieff (9 miles)

The line to Crieff was authorised in 1853 and opened to the public on 14 March 1856 by the Scottish Central Railway, later to become part of the Caledonian Railway. Stations were built at Tullibardine (2½ miles), Muthill (5 miles) and Highlandman (7½ miles). The passenger service was to Crieff with the occasional through working to St Fillans until the line beyond Comrie closed on 1 October 1951. The Caledonian renamed Crieff Junction in 1912 and the station became known as Gleneagles. Rebuilding took some time and Gleneagles was not completed until 1919. BR introduced four-wheeled railbuses in 1959 and opened two new rail-level halts. The passengers boarded the Wickham four-wheeler by means of fold-down steps, a practice not new on British railways as steam railmotors introduced from 1905 had pioneered the same system. The halts were located at Strageath (6¼ miles) and Pittenzie (8½ miles). The railbus experiment was not considered a success by the Scottish Region of BR and passenger services were withdrawn on 6 July 1964. Freight traffic was withdrawn from Crieff to Muthill from 2 November 1964, having been withdrawn from Muthill back to Gleneagles on 1 September 1964. Most of the trackbed is now a footpath and the station site at Crieff is now a health centre and ambulance station. Tullibardine and Highlandman stations are now private residences but Muthill has been built over.

Comrie on 29 July 1960 shows the four-wheeled railbus introduced on the line in 1959. The four-wheeled railbus was one of five built by D. Wickham & Co for the Scottish Region. The passenger service was withdrawn on 6 July 1964. *E. Wilmshurst*

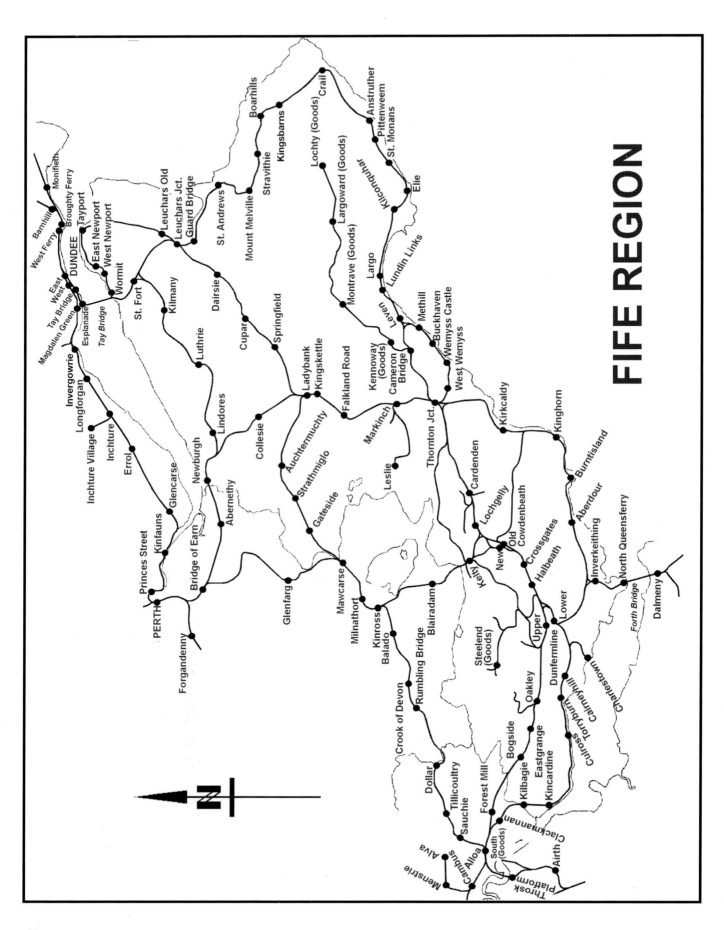

FIFE REGION

Fife

Leuchars Junction to Tay Bridge South (via Tayport) (10½ miles)

Tayport was the terminus for the ferry to Broughty Ferry on the north bank of the River Tay where the railway-owned steamers plied prior to the opening of the Tay Bridge. Leuchars to Tayport was opened by the Edinburgh & Northern Railway on 17 May 1848, having been authorised in 1846. The E&NR became part of the North British Railway by amalgamation at a later date. The ferry commenced operation in 1850 and was the first rail-tracked ferry. The direct line from Leuchars Old declined in importance after the opening of the Tay Bridge and the local service operated by the NBR became a mere four passenger trains per weekday which declined to three under the LNER. BR withdrew the Leuchars Junction to Tayport passenger trains on 9 January 1956 and closed the Leuchars Junction to Leuchars Old section to all traffic. Freights were discontinued back to Tayport by 23 May 1966.

The Tayport to Dundee section was more of a success as passengers could commute into Dundee. There were stations at East Newport (2½ miles from Tayport), West Newport (3¼ miles) and Wormit (4¾ miles). The line was opened on 13 May 1879 but was closed by BR on 18 December 1967 between Tayport and Newport-on-Tay and on 5 May 1969 from Newport-on-Tay East to Tay Bridge South to all traffic. The station building at Wormit was transferred to Bo'ness.

Tayport, with a Metro Cammell multiple-unit bound for Arbroath in the days before the line's closure to passengers, which was on 18 December 1967. In this 1961 photograph the original fixtures and fittings survive, including lower quadrant signals and well-kept flower beds. *Author*

Left:
The Easter 1962 'Scottish Rambler' stops briefly at Kilmany for photographs with 'J39' class No 64786, the Gresley post-Grouping 0-6-0 design dating from 1926. The train consists of five BR Mk 1 coaches in the standard maroon livery of the time. *Author*

Right:
LNER 'J39' 0-6-0 No 64786 waits at Luthrie on 22 April 1962 with the BLS/SLS 'Scottish Rambler' railtour. The North British black and white enamel nameboard has survived on the 1909 station. *Author*

Below:
Lindores on 22 April 1962 with the 'Scottish Rambler' hauled by Gresley 'J39' No 64786. The line was opened from St Fort to Newburgh on 25 January 1909 and worked by the NBR. BR closed the line on 12 February 1951 to passengers and Lindores to St Fort on 5 October 1964 to freight. *Author*

St Fort to Newburgh (Glenburnie Junction) (14½ miles)

The Edinburgh & Northern Railway (later NBR) opened the line to Perth on 18 July 1848 from Ladybank, the line having been authorised under an Act of 1845. What was later to become the BR main line from Edinburgh to Perth was closed to passengers on 9 September 1955 from Ladybank but reopened on 6 October 1975. At Glenburnie Junction the NBR line to Dundee joined the present main line which is now singled. The Newburgh & North Fife Railway opened its St Fort to Newburgh line on 25 January 1909 (NBR-worked) and provided intermediate stations at Kilmany (2¾ miles), Luthrie (6¾ miles) and Lindores (11¾ miles). A sparse service of three trains per weekday was provided on what was the NBR's Dundee to Perth service rivalling the more direct Caledonian route. The service had declined to just two trains per day by the time that the system had been Nationalised with BR withdrawing passenger trains on 12 February 1951. Freight traffic was withdrawn from Glenburnie to Lindores on 4 April 1960 and Lindores to St Fort on 5 October 1964. The line was visited by an SLS/BLS railtour on 22 April 1962 hauled by 'J39' class 0-6-0 No 64786. The stations were well preserved and the use of concrete in the platforms signified their fairly modern construction. Today, the station buildings have been removed but the station houses remain and were built to the Mansart design being very French in appearance. The Newburgh station building survives.

Abernethy with the 1960 Scottish railtour of SLS/RCTS fame shows NBR No 256 *Glen Douglas* of 1913 on 17 June 1960. The line was closed by BR on 19 September 1955 as the Ladybank to Perth branch but reopened on 6 October 1975 as the main line from Perth. The station, although closed with the line in 1955, was not reopened. *Author*

Two views of the long-abandoned Ladybank to Kinross line, opened as the Fife & Kinross Railway in March 1858. The line later became part of the North British system but BR withdrew passenger services on 5 June 1950. Freight traffic from Ladybank to Auchtermuchty ceased on 29 January 1957 and Auchtermuchty to Mawcarse on 6 October 1964. The first view shows Auchtermuchty with No 256 on 13 April 1963, the second shows Strathmiglo. *Author*

Ladybank to Mawcarse Junction (11½ miles)

The Fife & Kinross Railway was authorised on 16 July 1855 from Ladybank to Milnathort and opened in March 1858. The line was extended to Kinross on 20 August 1858. In 1862 the F&KR became part of the NBR. Stations were located at Auchtermuchty (4¾ miles), Strathmiglo (6¾ miles) and Gateside (8¾ miles). The NBR provided four trains per weekday with an extra on Saturdays, a service that was perpetuated into LNER days. BR withdrew the passenger trains on 5 June 1950 and freight from Ladybank to Auchtermuchty on 29 January 1957. Auchtermuchty to Mawcarse closed to all traffic on 6 October 1964. The line was visited on 17 June 1960 by the RCTS/SLS week-long tour of Scotland and again on 17 April 1963 by the BLS/SLS Easter tour. Mawcarse to Glenfarg on the old main line is now the M90 motorway. Some station buildings survive; Strathmiglo has been converted into a residence and Auchtermuchty is part of a factory. The old station house remains at Gateside.

Bridge of Earn to Cowdenbeath (22 miles)

The NBR main line from Perth to Edinburgh via Kinross is no longer in being as today's Edinburgh to Perth trains run via Ladybank. The Edinburgh & Northern Railway was authorised on 31 July 1845 from Burntisland to Perth via Thornton, Ladybank and Newburgh and opened throughout on 18 July 1848. Burntisland was the port on the Firth of Forth used by ferries until the Forth Bridge opened in 1890. Thornton Junction to Dunfermline opened on 13 December 1849. The Kinross-shire Railway was authorised on 10 August 1857 from Cowdenbeath to Kinross and opened on 20 June 1860. The KR became part of the NBR in 1862 by which time the railway had been connected up with the Fife & Kinross. The NBR opened the Mawcarse to Bridge of Earn section on 2 June 1890 to passengers as part of the new works associated with the Forth Bridge opening. The ex-NBR main line route from Bridge of Earn to Cowdenbeath was closed to passengers on 5 January 1970 and to all traffic to Milnathort. Freight traffic was withdrawn to Kelty from Milnathort on 4 May 1970 and back to Cowdenbeath North Junction on 12 July 1972. Several colliery branches existed in the area, including the Kelty to Redford Junction line via Westfield and Kinglassie completed by the LNER in 1925 and still open from Westfield to Redford Junction. This is all that remains of a once numerous system of colliery lines in Fifeshire, many of which closed in the 1960s. The Auchtertool branch (1896) closed back to Foulford Junction on 6 August 1962, having closed back from Invertiel Junction on 3 October 1960. Loch Leven up-side building is in use as a house.

Leslie was the terminus of a short branch from Markinch opened in 1857 by the NBR and closed on 4 January 1932 by the LNER to passengers. BR withdrew the freight on 9 October 1967. The daily goods is seen in the passenger platform in BR days, the old trackbed now having been turned into a walk known as the Boblingen Way. *C. H. A. Townley*

NBR No 64618 has arrived at Leslie with the Easter 1963 'Scottish Rambler' organised by the SLS and BLS. The spruced up 'J37' built by NBL in 1920 for the NBR lasted almost until the end of steam working in Scotland. *Author*

Markinch to Leslie (4¼ miles)

Opened in 1857 from the main line at Markinch, the branch had five passenger trains per weekday with two extras on Saturdays under the NBR. By 1922 the service had increased to seven trains per weekday with an extra on Saturdays but the LNER withdrew the passenger service on 4 January 1932. BR withdrew the freight on 9 October 1967. A branch to Auchtermuchty led off the Leslie branch but has been disused since 1990. Leslie station (now demolished) was visited on 13 April 1963 by the 'Scottish Rambler'. The Boblingen Way footpath now uses the old trackbed.

Thornton Junction to Methil (5¼ miles)

The Thornton to Buckhaven section of this line opened on 8 August 1881 and was extended to Methil on 5 May 1887. The North British took over the line and the dock at Methil in 1889. Coal from Fife was exported from Methil by the NBR via Thornton Junction but there was also the Wemyss Private Railway. The WPR had an extensive system linking the collieries with the port and had a fleet of Barclay 0-6-0Ts supplemented by Austerity 0-6-0STs. The railway escaped Nationalisation and continued to handle the coal traffic but a fire at Michael Colliery in 1967 killed off most of the traffic. The WPR closed in 1970 when the 'main line' of the system from Lochead to Denbeath was taken out of use following the closure of Lochead Colliery.

The NBR branch was provided with six trains per weekday and two extras on Saturdays serving West Wemyss (1 mile, closed in 1949), Wemyss Castle (2¾ miles) and Buckhaven (4 miles). The LNER was providing eight trains per weekday by 1947 but BR withdrew the passenger service on 10 January 1955. Freight traffic was withdrawn from Thornton Junction to West Wemyss on 2 December 1963 and Lochead to Methil on 15 October 1966. The railway from Thornton Junction is still in situ to Methil Power Station by way of Cameron Bridge. Methil station site has now been cleared and there is a health centre on the site of Buckhaven. West Wemyss has been demolished and Wemyss Castle survived until recently.

Methil East Junction with the 1962 RCTS/SLS Scottish railtour with 'J38' No 65905 running tender first with a five-coach train which includes the two preserved Caledonian corridors. The passenger service to Methil was withdrawn on 10 January 1955. *R. Hamilton*

Methil in LNER days shows an LNER Sentinel steam railcar at the terminus. The LNER out of the four pre-1948 railways used Sentinel steam railcars on a wide scale, the first being introduced in 1925 and the last in 1932. The LNER named its units after stage coaches and some survived until 1947. *Lens of Sutton*

Crail on 12 June 1960 with NBR No 256 *Glen Douglas* posing for photographs. The NBR signalbox is in the background and the signalman's stands can be seen at the edge of the platform slopes — an NBR practice. The line had closed to all traffic by 6 October 1969. *Author*

Leuchars Junction to Thornton Junction (via St Andrews) (39½ miles)

The Fife coast line of the former North British Railway was built piecemeal, the first section from Leuchars to St Andrews being opened to traffic on 1 July 1852. The 5¼-mile branch was authorised as the St Andrews Railway on 3 July 1851 and later taken into the NBR in 1877. The next part of the Fife coast line to be opened was from Thornton Junction to Leven on 3 July 1854. The Leven Railway was authorised by an Act of 17 June 1853, was 6 miles long and worked by the Edinburgh, Perth & Dundee Railway, later to become part of the NBR system. The East Fife Railway opened from Leven to Kilconquhar on 8 July 1857 and amalgamated with the Leven Railway on 22 July 1861 to become the Leven & East of Fife Railway. The L&EFR extended to Anstruther on 1 September 1863 but the gap to St Andrews was not filled until 1 June 1887 by the Anstruther & St Andrews Railway, later to be amalgamated with the NBR in 1897. The line passed through a coastal stretch before turning inland at Crail to run through agricultural countryside to St Andrews.

Stations were provided at Cameron Bridge (3¾ miles), Leven (5¾ miles), Lundin Links, 7¾ miles), Largo (8¾ miles), Kilconquhar (13½ miles), Elie (14 miles), St Monance (16¼ miles), Pittenweem (17¾ miles), Anstruther (18¾ miles), Crail (23 miles), Kingsbarns (26 miles), Boarhills (27½ miles), Stravithie (29¾) Mt Melville (32 miles), St Andrews (34 miles) and Guard Bridge (37¾ miles). The LNER had a purge in 1930 and closed four intermediate stations between Crail and St Andrews to passengers on 20 September 1930. The line was worked in two sections as far as the passenger traffic was concerned with a fairly frequent service from St Andrews to Dundee and four through trains to Thornton with seven from Crail in NBR days. A through express, the 'Fifeshire Coast Express' (1910-59) was run from Aberdeen to Glasgow by this route. The line was closed to all traffic from Leuchars Junction back to Leven East Fife Central Junction by 6 October 1969. Most of the stations have been demolished but the station house survives at Stravithie as does the platform at Kingsbarns. Crail station building survives as part of a garden centre and Largo viaduct is intact.

Lochty was a goods only branch of the former NBR and was 14¾ miles in length. The scene here is at the terminus and shows the branch 'J36' class 0-6-0 No 65345 shunting out empty wagons. The engine was fitted with a tender cab and snowplough and together with No 65288 of the same class was the last steam engine in use on the Region. *R. Hamilton*

Leven to Lochty (14¾ miles)

The East Fife Central Railway, worked by the NBR, was authorised on 24 August 1893 and opened on 21 August 1898. The branch did not have a passenger service but had intermediate goods stations at Kennoway, Montrave and Largoward. The single-track branch left the main line at East Fife Central Junction, 1¼ miles from Leven on the Fife Coast route. The traffic in seed potatoes kept the line busy at certain times of the year but freight ceased to run after 10 August 1964. The railway's claim to fame was that it was the home of Gresley 'A4' class 4-6-2 No 60009 *Union of South Africa* for many years before the engine was released for main line

service in 1971. The engine worked on a short stretch of track at the Lochty end of the line. The Lochty Private Railway started operations in 1967 and ran on Sunday afternoons to Knightsward, a distance of 1¼ miles. A Peckett 0-4-0ST and an Austerity 0-6-0ST together with a Ruston & Hornsby diesel shunter worked the service on the top end of the line purchased by John Cameron from BR after closure. The Lochty goods engine, Class J36 0-6-0 No 65345, was fitted with a snowplough and, together with No 65288 of the same class, had the distinction of being the last steam locomotive to be in use on the Scottish Region in 1967.

An early view of Charlestown which
opened to passengers on
1 September 1894. The station has
the usual collection of enamel
advertising of the period.
Commercial card

Dunfermline and Charlestown (4¼ miles)

The Charlestown Railway originally started as a horse-worked tramway to take coal down to the coast. A system of colliery railways from the pits around Dunfermline having developed in the late 18th century. The North British rebuilt the Elgin Railway and opened the Charlestown branch to passengers on 1 September 1894. The NBR provided seven passenger trains per weekday between Dunfermline Lower and Charlestown. The service had increased to 11 trains by the Grouping and included a halt at Braeside but the line was closed to passengers on 1 November 1926. BR closed the line to freight on 24 February 1964. The station was converted into a private house but was completely rebuilt.

The Charlestown goods consisting of mineral wagons loaded with scrap is headed by 'J36' class No 65253 of the NBR. This engine was built by Sharp, Stewart & Co for the NBR in February 1892 and withdrawn by BR in May 1963. Twenty-five members of the class were named by the NBR in 1919 and No 65253, formerly No 682, was named *Joffre. W. S. Sellar*

Charlestown in LNER days after closure to passengers which occurred on 1 November 1926, the line surviving until 24 February 1964 for freight traffic. An old coach body has been placed on the platform for storage purposes. *Lens of Sutton*

Inverkeithing to Rosyth Dockyard (2¼ miles)

A passenger service operated to Rosyth Dockyard from Kirkcaldy and Edinburgh. Two trains ran in the morning and returned in the late afternoon. The service was not advertised and was provided for dockyard workers. There was an intermediate station at Limpetness, 1¼ miles from Inverkeithing Central. The line closed to all traffic in March 1990 following the dockyard closure. The North Queensferry branch was closed to all traffic on 4 October 1954.

Dunfermline sees ex-North British 'J37' 0-6-0 No 64569 heading towards Alloa with a loaded coal train on 28 May 1966. The engine was built at Cowlairs in 1918 and was withdrawn shortly after this picture was taken, steam finishing in Scotland the following year. *Author*

Central

Alloa to Kinross Junction (17 miles)

The first section of the Devon Valley line was opened on 3 June 1851, from Alloa to Tillicoultry, by the Stirling & Dunfermline Railway under an Act of 16 July 1846. The section from Kinross to Rumbling Bridge was opened by the Devon Valley Railway on 1 May 1863 under an Act of 1858 and worked by the North British. The Rumbling Bridge to Tillicoultry section was completed on 1 May 1871 and the local company merged with the NBR in 1875. Stations were provided at Sauchie (1½ miles), Tillicoultry (3½ miles), Dollar (6¼ miles), Rumbling Bridge (10½ miles), Crook of Devon (12 miles) and Balado (15 miles). Sauchie was closed by the LNER on 22 September 1930. The original station at Kinross was replaced in 1890 by a new station on a different site north of the junction. The NBR provided through trains including a Glasgow to Perth service which was perpetuated by the LNER. Under BR the passenger service was reduced with some trains starting from Dollar for Stirling. The line survived longer than most cross-country branches with passenger trains being withdrawn on 15 June 1964. BR withdrew the freight from Kinross to Dollar on 20 April 1964 and Dollar to Alloa on 25 June 1973. Dollar to Tillicoultry is earmarked for the Hillfoots Walk. Most of the stations on the line have been demolished since closure.

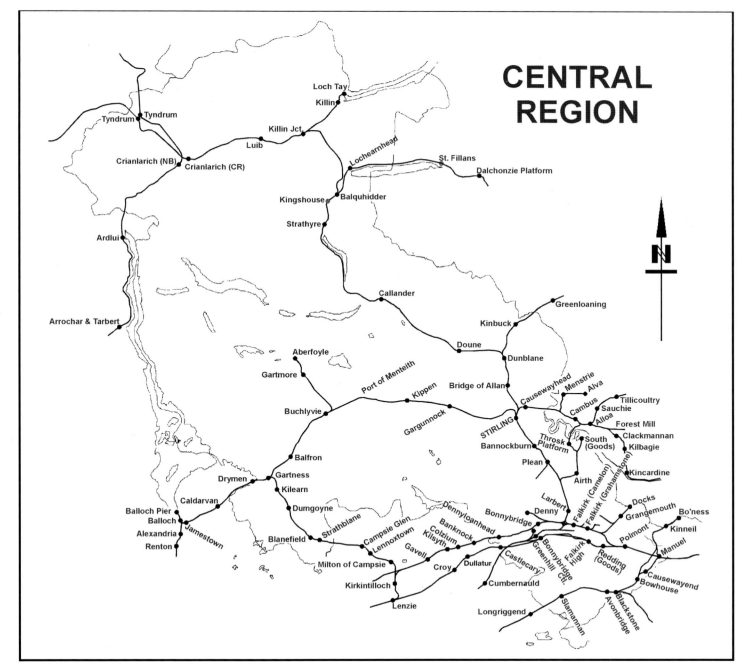

Above:
Alloa East signalbox on 27 May 1966 with a 'WD' class 2-8-0 heading towards Dunfermline with a trainload of empties for the Fife pits. The loco shed with a Gresley 'J38' is visible through the arch of the road bridge. On the cattle dock can be seen a fine assortment of period railwaymen's cars. *Author*

Above right:
A scene that was once commonplace in the industrial parts of Britain with ex-LNER 'J38' class 0-6-0 No 65912 drifting along with a loaded coal train near Alloa in May 1966. Steam had only a year to go before abolition on the region. *Author*

Right:
'J38' class No 65912 brings mineral empties into Alloa for the Fifeshire pits on 27 May 1966. Alloa is now without a passenger service but there is a proposal to reopen the line to Stirling for passenger traffic which will include stations at Cambus and Causewayhead. *Author*

A few of the former LNER 'B1' class 4-6-0s were named. No 61029 *Chamois* heads coal empties to the Fife pits on 28 May 1966 and is seen near Kincardine Junction. The Thompson 'B1' class originated in 1942 and 409 examples were built under the LNER and BR(ER). Two examples have been preserved. *Author*

A scene on the Devon Valley line in May 1958 shows the ex-North British signalbox situated on the embankment. The point rods extend from underneath the signalbox and drop down to ground level by an unusual means. The passenger service was withdrawn on 15 June 1964. *Author*

The 'Scottish Rambler' has arrived at Alva on 3 April 1963 and NBR 'J36' No 65323 has run round the train ready for departure to Cambus. The 'J36' was built at Cowlairs in 1900 by the NBR and withdrawn by BR in December 1963. The branch closed to all traffic on 2 March 1964. *Author*

Cambus to Alva (3½ miles)

The Alva Railway Co was opened on 3 June 1863 having been authorised on 22 July 1861. The line was worked by the Edinburgh & Glasgow Railway, later to become part of the North British system. The line was going to be extended to Tillicoultry on the Devon Valley but the extension was never built. The curiosity about this branch was that the distance from Alva to Alloa was 5½ miles by rail as distinct from 2½ miles by road. Once the motorbus had got going there was not much chance for the passenger service but it did survive until 1 November 1954 under BR. The NBR provided 11 trains per day which was similar to that of the LNER before 1948. There was one intermediate station at Menstrie, two miles from Cambus, the junction station. BR withdrew the freight from Alva on 2 March 1964, the traffic from Menstrie distillery providing much revenue during its heyday. Alva station has been cleared and converted into a car park but platform remains can be discerned at Menstrie and Cambus.

Stirling to Dunfermline (Upper) (20½ miles)

The Stirling & Dunfermline Railway was authorised under an Act of 16 July 1846 and was opened throughout on 1 July 1852. The Edinburgh & Glasgow Railway took over the S&DR in 1858 and the line subsequently became part of the NBR in 1865. Stations were located at Causewayhead (1¼ miles), Cambus (4¾ miles), Alloa (6¾ miles), Clackmannan Road (9 miles), Forest Mill (10 miles), Bogside (12½ miles), East Grange (14½ miles) and Oakley (16 miles). Twelve trains per weekday were provided by the NBR including through trains from Stirling to Edinburgh on what was then the NBR main line.

Causewayhead closed to passengers on 4 July 1955, Clackmannan Road on 1 December 1921, Forest Mill on 22 September 1930, Bogside on 2 January 1967, East Grange on 15 September 1958 and Oakley, along with the passenger service from Stirling to Dunfermline, on 7 October 1968. Quite a range of passenger closures for a former main line! Freight traffic was withdrawn by BR and the through route out of use by 1980 but the Alloa to Stirling section is proposed for reopening to passenger traffic. The overgrown track is still in situ at Alloa but the rest of the stations through to Dunfermline have been demolished, except Bogside which is now a house with a cycleway running along the old trackbed.

Alloa to Dunfermline (Lower) (via Kincardine) (17¼ miles)

The North British opened the coast line to Kincardine on 18 December 1893 and continued on to Dunfermline on 30 June 1906. The line was worked in two sections based on Kincardine with four trains to Dunfermline and five trains per weekday to Alloa with extras on Saturdays. The LNER withdrew passenger trains on 7 July 1930 but freight lasted longer, in fact the line is still in use from Dunfermline to serve Longannet Power Station. The NBR built stations at Clackmannan (2 miles), Kilbagie (3¾ miles), Kincardine (5½ miles), Culross (10¼ miles), Torryburn (12 miles) and Cairneyhill (13¼ miles). BR closed the Alloa to Kincardine section to regular freight on 6 April 1981. The stations have been demolished but Kincardine may reopen in the future through to Alloa and Stirling.

Alloa to Larbert (8½ miles)

The Scottish Central Railway opened a branch from the main line at Alloa Junction to South Alloa on 12 September 1850 under an Act of 1846. A ferry was provided to take passengers across the River Forth. The SCR was amalgamated into the Caledonian in 1865 and Alloa Junction station closed in November of that year. Airth station, 1½ miles from Alloa Junction, was opened in 1866 and the bridge over the Forth on 1 October 1885. A halt at Throsk on the south side of the bridge was opened in 1890 to serve the seven Caledonian trains per weekday which ran to Glasgow. Passenger services were withdrawn by the Scottish Region on 29 January 1968 and the bridge closed from 6 May 1968. The Throsk to Alloa Junction section closed to freight on 1 April 1978, the bridge having been demolished in 1971. The station building at Airth has been demolished but the rebuilt station house is now a cattery.

Falkirk to Grangemouth (5¾ miles)

The railway to Grangemouth was originally built by the Forth & Clyde Canal Co and was opened for goods in 1860 and passengers in 1861. The Caledonian Railway purchased the Forth & Clyde in 1867 and as a result inherited the branch to Grangemouth. A cut-off line was opened in 1908 bypassing Grahamston to join the original Grangemouth branch at Fouldubs Junction. The North British and the Caledonian Railways both ran a passenger service to Glasgow and the line prospered, the joint service lasting until LNER and LMS days. Under BR an approximately hourly service ran to Glasgow but the passenger service was withdrawn on 29 January 1968. Today, the line flourishes with oil and coal traffic, the avoiding line to Fouldubs Junction having closed after the passenger withdrawal. The passenger station at Grahamston has been demolished.

The driver and guard pose in front of the diesel multiple-unit at Grangemouth on 31 August 1961. The station had an overall roof and a single platform. The passenger service was withdrawn on 29 January 1968 but the line is still busy with freight traffic to the port. *Author*

Manuel Low Level, seen in a semi-derelict state, was an important interchange point in pre-Grouping days with trains from Glasgow and Bathgate terminating underneath the main line. Passenger services were withdrawn by the LNER on 5 May 1930 but the high level station on the main line survived until 6 March 1967 under BR.
Lens of Sutton

Bo'ness on the last day of passenger operation with Ivatt 2-6-0 No 43141 on 3 May 1956. BR closed the line to all traffic on 19 July 1965. The present Bo'ness & Kinneil Railway starts at a different terminus and was opened on 27 July 1981.
W. A. C. Smith

Manuel to Bo'ness (4¼ miles)

Bo'ness was reached by rail from Causewayend by the Slamannan & Borrowstounness Railway where the promoters planned to lease the harbour. The railway was opened on 17 March 1851 under an Act of 1846 but traffic did not reach the expectations of the promoters. The line, as part of the Monkland Railway, became part of the NBR and the NBR provided a passenger service of 12 trains per weekday. There was an intermediate station at Kinneil, 3¼ miles from Manuel. The LNER diverted the service to Polmont but in its 1947 timetable there is a very curious note in that theatrical traffic will not be conveyed by the 7.42am Bo'ness for transfer at Polmont to the 7.36am Glasgow to Thornton'. The LNER was at the time running 10 trains per weekday. The Scottish Region withdrew the passenger service on 7 May 1956 and freight on 19 July 1965 back to Kinneil Colliery. The line back to Bo'ness Junction from Kinneil was closed to all traffic on 16 July 1979. In 1979 the Scottish Railway Preservation Society took a lease on land from Falkirk District Council and started to build a new

Bo'ness station half-a-mile from the old NBR station. The new station opened on 27 July 1981 and trains operated on a short length of track until Kinneil was reached in 1985. The Bo'ness & Kinneil Railway now extends to Birkhill where a connection extends to Bo'ness Junction on the main line. The Victorian building at Bo'ness originated from Wormit and the train shed from Haymarket.

Larbert to Denny (3¾ miles)

The Denny branch of the Caledonian Railway was opened to traffic on 1 April 1858. The CR provided a passenger service to Larbert which, by 1923, consisted of eight trains per weekday with extras on Saturdays. In 1888 a south curve was put in at Denny West Junction to enable trains to run to Greenhill and Glasgow. The NBR/Caledonian joint line arrived on the scene on 2 July 1888 with its branch from Kilsyth to Bonnywater Junction 1¾ miles from Denny. The LMS withdrew the passenger service from Denny and Bonnybridge (CR) on 28 July 1930. Freight had ceased on the branch by 3 April 1972.

The Branch Line Society has reached Denny with a special train of authentic Caledonian stock hauled by Pickersgill 4-4-0 No 54465. The branch was closed to passenger traffic by the LMS on 28 July 1930 and freight by BR on 3 April 1972. *W. A. C. Smith*

Denny on 17 June 1960 with ex-NBR 4-4-0 No 256 *Glen Douglas* on the RCTS/SLS week's railtour of Scotland. The stock consisted of the two ex-Caledonian coaches, a GER buffet, a BR Mk 1 in red and cream and a Gresley open tourist second. *Author*

Kilsyth with an SLS railtour on 3 May 1958 headed by ex-NBR 'J36' No 65315. The line was closed by the LNER to passengers on 1 February 1935 and by BR to freight on 4 May 1964. *Author*

Kilsyth with the 'J36' on 3 May 1958 which has run round the train prior to returning to Glasgow with the SLS railtour. The train consists of a magnificent Gresley six-coach set in ex-works condition resplendent in maroon — the standard BR livery from 1956. *Author*

Bonnybridge to Greenhill (¾ mile)

The short Caledonian branch to Bonnybridge opened to passenger traffic on 2 August 1886 and a meagre service of three trains per weekday was provided (with an extra on Saturdays) which had declined to two by 1923. The service was withdrawn by the LMS on 28 July 1930, the same day as that from the Denny branch. BR used the line for freight until 7 December 1964.

Larbert to Kilsyth (10 miles)

The Kilsyth & Bonnybridge joint line was opened for traffic on 2 July 1888 from Bonnywater Junction near Denny to Kilsyth under an Act of 1887. At Kilsyth a new station was built to connect with the NBR from Glasgow. Stations were built at Bonnybridge Central (3¼ miles from Larbert), Dennyloanhead (4¾ miles), Banknock (6 miles) and Colzium (9 miles). The Caledonian ran a service of three trains per weekday and the North British four, through to Glasgow from Bonnybridge. The passenger service was withdrawn on 1 February 1935, the section to Dennyloanhead being closed to all traffic from Bonnywater Junction. Freight was withdrawn back to Banknock on 1 March 1956 and finally Kilsyth on 4 May 1964.

Lenzie Junction to Aberfoyle (28 miles)

The first section of what was to become the North British Aberfoyle branch was opened to Lennoxtown by the Edinburgh & Glasgow Railway on 5 July 1848 under an Act of 1845. The next section to be opened was to Killearn on 1 July 1867. The line was worked by the NBR from the outset and ran from a new station at Lennoxtown, thus creating Lennoxtown Old as well as the new Blane Valley establishment. The 'Old' station became a goods depot from 1881. Extension from Killearn northwards was achieved on 1 October 1882 when the line was opened to Gartness Junction and Aberfoyle under an Act of 1880. The section from Gartness Junction to Buchlyvie had already been completed by the Forth & Clyde Junction Railway, opened in 1856 and also worked by the NBR. The stations on the line were located at Kirkintilloch (8 miles from Glasgow), Milton of Campsie (9¾ miles), Lennoxtown (11½ miles), Campsie Glen (12½ miles), Strathblane (15¾ miles), Blanefield (16¾ miles), Dumgoyne (19¾ miles), Killearn (21¼ miles), Balfron (F&C 24¼ miles), Buchlyvie (F&C 28½ miles), Gartmore (32½ miles, closed 1950) and Aberfoyle (34¼ miles). Aberfoyle was a single-platformed terminus with an engine shed and goods shed. There was a coach connection to the Trossachs which was provided by the LNER until September 1939. The NBR provided five trains per weekday including three through from Glasgow Queen St. Two extra trains were run on Saturdays and a through service was being run to Edinburgh in the summer of 1922 by the NBR. The LNER had a measly three trains per weekday with an extra on Saturdays prior to Nationalisation in 1948. Back O'Loch Halt, opened by the LNER in 1925, was located half a mile before Kirkintilloch and served the suburbs of that town. BR withdrew the passenger service from Aberfoyle to Kirkintilloch on 1 October 1951. Freight was withdrawn from Campsie Glen to Aberfoyle on 5 October 1959, back to Lennoxtown on 28 September 1964 and Kirkintilloch on 4 April 1966. A railtour was run by the SLS on Saturday, 3 May 1958 from Glasgow Queen Street to Aberfoyle and back-hauled by ex-NBR 'J36' class No 65316 on what was probably the last passenger train. The Kirkintilloch to Lenzie section closed to passengers on 7 September 1964 and freight on 4 April 1966. A footpath runs southwards from Aberfoyle for one mile. The site of the station is now occupied by a car park and at Gartmore and Buchlyvie the station houses survive. Gartness to Blanefield is now a long distance walk; Balfron, Killearn and Blanefield have been demolished but Dumgoyne is now a house. The rest of the stations down the branch to Kirkintilloch have been demolished. The old trackbed south of Strathblane to Lenzie will be converted into a footpath.

North British 'J36' No 65315 eases the SLS railtour into Lennoxtown so slowly that the author has jumped off the train and run ahead of it to photograph the train arriving! A few locals have turned out to see a passenger train on the line where the service was withdrawn on 1 October 1951. *Author*

Above:
Ex-North British 0-6-0 No 65315 of 1899 crosses the road at Blanefield on 3 May 1958 with the SLS special to Aberfoyle. Some of the engines in the ex-NBR 'C' class were named after service in France during World War 1. *Author*

Above right:
Dumgoyne on the former branch to Aberfoyle on 3 May 1958 with NBR 'J36' No 65315 on the SLS special. A fine collection of period motor cars has drawn up to let the special pass. *Author*

Right:
Aberfoyle was the terminus of the ex-NBR 28-mile line from Lenzie. The area was a popular venue for day trippers and tourists going to the Trossochs and the scene here depicts a special hauled by ex-LNER 'K4' class 2-6-0 No 61998 *Macleod of Macleod,* one of a class of six engines introduced by Gresley in 1937 for the West Highland line. An example of the class, No 61994 *The Great Marquess,* has been preserved. Note the ex-LNER beaver-tail observation car next to the engine. *W. A. C. Smith*

Above:
Loch Tay station in June 1957 was not in use but the engine, CR 0-4-4T No 55126, had to run down the branch from Killin to take water. The passenger station, closed on 11 September 1939 when the steamers were withdrawn, is now a house. NBR coaches can be seen with loco coal wagons in the siding. *Author*

Right:
Ex-Caledonian 0-4-4T No 55126 rests outside Loch Tay shed on 1 June 1957. The engine was one of the McIntosh '92' class introduced in 1897 for working branch lines and suburban passenger trains. The engine was originally fitted with condensing gear for Glasgow low level lines. *Author*

Stirling to Balloch (30¼ miles)

The Forth & Clyde Junction Railway was opened for traffic on 26 May 1856 and was authorised on 4 August 1853. The purpose of the promoters was to enable the railway to take export coal and pig iron from Fife to the River Clyde. The Forth Bridge was not opened until 1890 and the F&CJR provided direct access to the Clyde. The railway was worked by the NBR which leased the line from 1875, the F&CJR not losing its identity until 1923. Stations were built at Gargunnock (6 miles from Stirling), Kippen (9 miles), Ladylands Siding (11¼ miles), Port of Menteith (13 miles), Buchlyvie (15¾ miles), Balfron (19¾ miles), Gartness (22 miles), Drymen (23½ miles), Caldarvan (26½ miles) and Jamestown (29½ miles). The NBR provided four through passenger trains per weekday with an extra from Balloch to Drymen on Saturdays. From 1882 Buchlyvie and Balfron were served by Aberfoyle to Glasgow trains which ran until 1 October 1951. The LNER withdrew the Stirling and Balloch passenger service on 1 October 1934 but freight traffic lasted longer, the sections from Buchlyvie to Port of Menteith and Gartness Junction to Drymen closing to all traffic on 1 November 1950. Port of Menteith to Stirling and Drymen to Jamestown closed to freight on 5 October 1959. Jamestown to Balloch finally closed on 1 September 1964. Kippen station is now a house with the signalbox in use as a greenhouse and Port of Menteith and Drymen are now houses, but Caldarvan is derelict. Jamestown has been demolished and Gargunnock has been built over.

Killin Junction to Loch Tay (5 miles)

The Caledonian main line reached Killin Junction on 1 June 1870 and was extended to Tyndrum in August 1873 while Oban was eventually reached in 1880. The 5-mile branch to Killin and Loch Tay was opened on 13 March 1886 having been promoted locally by the Marquis of Breadalbane and authorised in 1883. The line consisted of a gradient of 1 in 50 for five miles. Steamers connected with the railway at Loch Tay where the locomotive was stabled in a one-road shed. The CR built two locomotives for the branch known as 'Killin Pugs'. They were 0-4-2 saddle tanks built at St Rollox Works and were replaced by 0-4-4 Drummond tanks in 1889. CR 0-4-4Ts worked the line for many years until BR Class 4 2-6-4Ts were introduced. Six passenger trains per day were run, making a connection at Killin Junction. The line to Loch Tay lost its passenger service on 11 September 1939 when the steamers were withdrawn. BR withdrew trains from Killin to Killin Junction on 28 September 1965 following a landslide at Glenogle on the main line. Killin to Loch Tay is now a footpath with Killin station site in use as a car park, the site at Killin Junction is a coniferous plantation and Loch Tay station is a house.

Killin on 12 April 1963 with Standard Class 4 2-6-4T No 80093 which had replaced the old CR 0-4-4Ts. The branch was closed to all traffic on 28 September 1965 following the landslide in Glenogle.
Author

Caley '2P' 0-4-4T No 55195 works the goods on the Killin branch on 5 May 1959. The old trackbed of this 5-mile branch is now a footpath between Killin and Loch Tay with the old station site at Killin in use as a car park.
E. Wilmshurst

Strathclyde

Dalreoch to Balloch Pier (4½ miles)

Opened on 15 July 1850 by the Dunbartonshire Railway, the passengers commenced their journey from Glasgow by steamer to board the connecting train at Bowling. From Balloch steamers plied to Inverarnan on Loch Lomond. On 26 May 1856 the Forth & Clyde Junction Railway opened from Stirling and made a connection at Balloch at the appropriately named Forth & Clyde Junction, ¼-mile south of the station. From 1 October 1896 the line became part of the 6-mile Dumbarton & Balloch Joint shared between the two

rivals, the NBR and the CR. The joint railway also operated the ships on Loch Lomond. Today, the branch is thriving, and having been singled by BR, is now part of the Strathclyde suburban system with a half-hourly service of electric trains on all days. The Balloch and Helensburgh Central services use the same track from Dalreoch, Helensburgh Central being a 1¼-mile branch from Craigendoran Junction on the West Highland route. The electric service was introduced on 5 November 1960 but failed initially and was reintroduced in 1961.

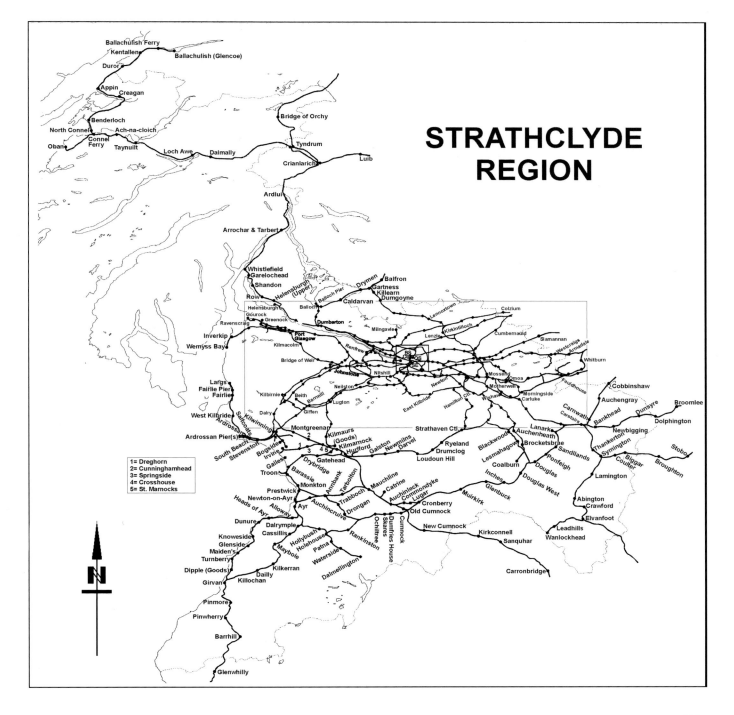

Westerton to Milngavie (3¼ miles)

Opened on 28 July 1863 with two intermediate stations, at Bearsden (1 mile) and later Hillfoot (1½ miles), the Milngavie line had an approximately half-hourly service under the NBR on weekdays only. The service was more or less the same under the LNER but the revolution came on 5 November 1960 with electrification and trains now run from Springburn to Milngavie, every half-hour on weekdays.

Kilsyth to Maryhill (11¼ miles)

The Kelvin Valley Railway was authorised on 21 July 1873 from Kilsyth to Maryhill with the intention of conveying export coal to the Clyde docks. The NBR built a connecting line from Lenzie to Kilsyth which was opened on 1 June 1878 and extended to Maryhill on 4 June 1879. The KVR was amalgamated into the NBR on 1 August 1885 and a passenger service of four trains per weekday ran from Kilsyth to Glasgow with an additional five starting from Torrance. Stations on the line were located at Gavell (1¼ miles), Torrance (6¼ miles), Balmore (7½ miles), Bardowie (8¾ miles), Summerston (9¼ miles) and Maryhill (11¼ miles). BR withdrew the passenger service on 31 March 1951. The freight traffic ceased on 24 June 1956 from Kelvin Valley East Junction to Torrance, on 5 October 1959 back to Balmore and on 31 July 1964 to Maryhill. Kilsyth Old was visited by the SLS railtour on 3 May 1958 with what was probably the last passenger train. The section from Kilsyth back to Twechar was closed to freight on 4 May 1964 and Kirkintilloch Junction on 4 April 1966. Kilsyth Old and New, Twechar and Balmore stations have been cleared but Torrance station house remains in situ. Bardowie and Summerston are derelict sites but Maryhill was reopened in 1994.

The Caledonian single was a unique engine and between 1958 and 1966 worked specials for railway clubs on the Scottish Region. No 123, built in 1886 by Neilson & Co for the Caledonian Railway, was the only engine of its class and the only 4-2-2 to run in Scotland. No 123 took part in the 1888 'Race to the North' and was withdrawn by the LMS in 1935. The engine is now in the Glasgow Transport Museum but is seen here passing Possil CR on 12 April 1963. *Author*

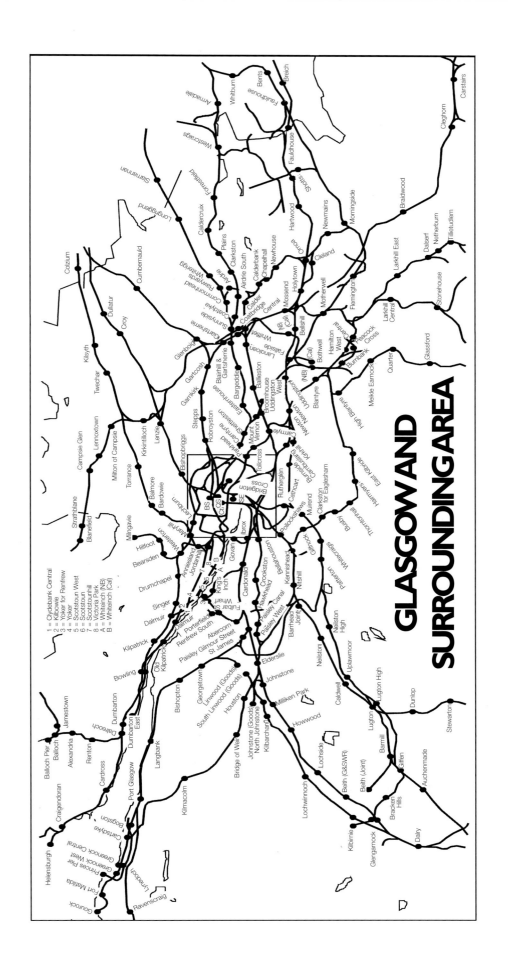

GLASGOW AND SURROUNDING AREA

1 = Clydebank Central
2 = Kilbowie
3 = Yoker for Renfrew
4 = Yoker
5 = Scotstoun West
6 = Scotstoun
7 = Scotstounhill
8 = Victoria Park
A = Whiteinch (NB)
B = Whiteinch (Cal)

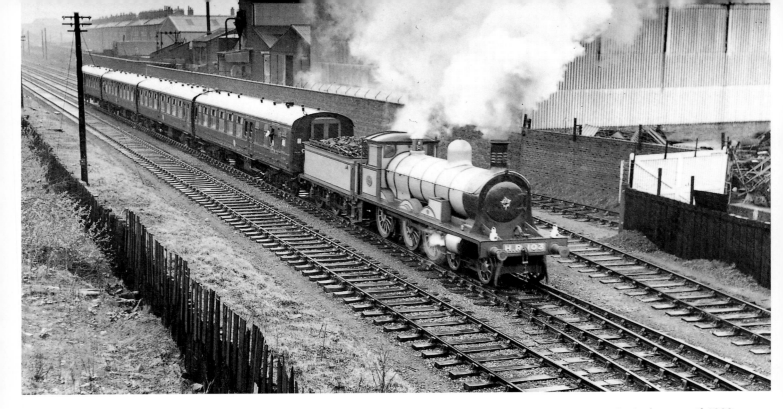

The Govan branch of the former Glasgow & Paisley Joint Railway had a busy passenger service to Springburn until 1902 when tramway competition killed it off. Workmen's trains ran until 1921 and freight trains ran until 5 September 1966. Govan station site was incorporated into an underground depot in 1979. The 'Jones Goods' of 1894 negotiates the ¾-mile branch with the 'Scottish Rambler' on 17 April 1965. *Author*

Glasgow Terminals

Apart from the obvious closures of Glasgow Buchanan Street (7 November 1966) and St Enoch (27 June 1966) there were one or two other 'bolt holes' in the city where suburban trains terminated. The North British ran passenger trains from a terminus at Whiteinch (Victoria Park) to Springburn and even a through train to Milngavie via Springburn and Maryhill. The LNER ran through trains from Victoria Park to Bridgeton Cross another short 1-mile-long branch on the eastern side of the city. Victoria Park lasted under BR for passengers until 2 April 1951 and Bridgeton Cross until 5 November 1979. A through service was run from Clydebank East to Airdrie and Hamilton and even Bridgeton Cross. The ¾-mile branch to Clydebank East lasted until 14 September 1959. The 52-chain Hyndland branch accommodated trains from Hamilton and Airdrie and lasted until 5 November 1960 when electrification brought about the construction of a rolling stock maintenance depot. The old Caley line from Maryhill to Stobcross closed on 2 November 1959 to passengers and 1964 to freight, the Possil to Partick section closing to passengers on 5 October 1964 and freight on 31 January 1966. Possil (CR) to Balornock Junction closed to freight on 18 October 1965. Parts of the old Caley system are earmarked for the new projected Strathclyde tram system — bring back the trams! On the south side of the Clyde the ¾-mile Govan branch of the G&PJ had a passenger service to Springburn until 1902, workmen's and excursions until 9 October 1921 and freight until 5 September 1966. The site was incorporated into an underground depot in 1979. The Bridgeton Cross to Coatbridge passenger service ceased on 5 October 1964 (via

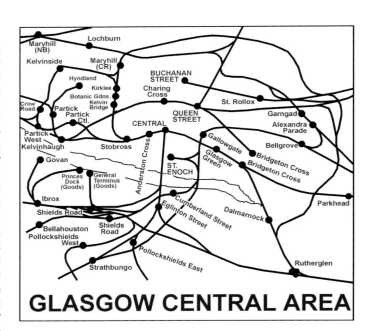

Carmyle). Freight traffic ceased over the Rutherglen to Balornock section on 7 September 1964. Possil CR platforms have survived with the buildings at street level, there is a supermarket on the site of Maryhill CR and the platforms and street level buildings survive at Kelvinside. Bridgeton Cross, Victoria Park and Clydebank East NB stations have been cleared.

The 'Jones Goods' shuffles along the former Caledonian Chain Road branch with the Easter 'Scottish Rambler' on 17 April 1965. The first 4-6-0 to run in Britain, No 103 is now preserved in the Glasgow Transport Museum. *Author*

The 'Jones Goods' passes Renfrew South with the 'Scottish Rambler' on 17 April 1965. The line, originally owned by the G&SWR, had a workmen's service until withdrawn by BR on 5 June 1967. *Author*

Paisley to Renfrew Wharf (3½ miles)

The first railway on the scene was the Paisley & Renfrew from Hamilton Street to Renfrew Wharf opened on 3 April 1837, and later to become part of the Glasgow, Paisley, Kilmarnock & Ayr Railway. The P&RR ran from Hamilton Street and was originally built to a gauge of 4ft 6in. The railway was converted from steam to horse traction in 1842 and was worked as such until taken over by the G&SWR in 1852. The G&SWR converted the track to standard gauge in 1866 and connected it to the main line at Gallowhill Junction. A direct service was put on to Glasgow by the G&SWR and Hamilton Street terminus closed. Stations were built at Abercorn (7¼ miles from Glasgow), South Renfrew (9 miles), Renfrew Fulbar Street (9¾ miles) and Renfrew Wharf (10¼ miles). The G&SWR service in 1922 was 11 trains on Mondays to Fridays and eight on Saturdays running direct to St Enoch. South Renfrew dated from 1897 and a halt entitled Sandyford Halt was opened in 1914 to serve the works of Ogston & Tennant situated 1¼ miles north of Abercorn. The service, which was provided for workmen, was withdrawn by BR on 5 June 1967. Freight lasted until 11 June 1978 from Renfrew Wharf back to Renfrew South. Little remains to be seen of the stations today.

Cardonald to Renfrew Porterfield (4¼ miles)

The joint branch to Renfrew was opened on 1 June 1903 to passengers and included an intermediate station at Kings Inch, 1¼ miles from Porterfield. The service from St Enoch consisted of seven trains on Mondays to Fridays and five on Saturdays. The passenger service was withdrawn by the LMS on 19 July 1926 and freight terminated from 6 July 1964. A connection was put in between the two branches in 1916 at Renfrew South. There was a station at Deanside from 1903 to 1905 and the line is still in situ from Cardonald Junction to Deanside distribution depot.

West Paisley to Barrhead Central (3¼ miles)

The G&SWR main line from Glasgow to Elderslie was opened on 1 July 1885. The G&SWR extended from Paisley West Junction (Corsebar Junction) to Potterhill and opened the line to passengers on 1 June 1886 under an Act of 1882. The line was extended to Barrhead Central and opened on 1 October 1902. A through service was run from Glasgow to Glasgow via Barrhead by the G&SWR until 1907. Potterhill station, 1½ miles from West Paisley, was served by a shuttle service from Barrhead Central until 1 June 1913. Both Potterhill and Barrhead G&SWR stations were closed to passengers on 1 January 1917 under wartime economies. Potterhill as a goods depot lasted until 2 March 1970 when the branch back to West Paisley was closed to all traffic. The main line today terminates at Paisley Canal, the part on to Elderslie having closed to all traffic on 10 March 1984. Barrhead Central has disappeared but Potterhill is now a house.

Paisley St James to Patterton (Lyon Cross Junction) (8½ miles)

The Paisley & Barrhead District Railway was authorised under an Act of 1897 and taken over by the Caledonian in 1902. Construction was started in 1898 and stations were built at Ferguslie, Stanely and Glenfield with plans for Barrhead New and South, Paisley East and Dykebar. The latter two were located on the 2¾-mile branch which left the 'main line' at Blackbyres Junction. The line opened to goods traffic in June 1905 but the passenger service was not implemented, for trams took all the traffic potential in the area and the CR decided to keep the line for goods only. BR closed the section from Barrhead South to Ferguslie on 28 October 1963 and Ferguslie to Rootes Siding on 30 September 1968. Paisley East traffic ceased on 30 June 1958. The Caley Linwood Goods branch from Blackstone Junction closed to freight traffic on 6 November 1967. Stanely and Glenfield were used as houses and let out by BR but have been demolished.

Upper Port Glasgow on 17 April 1965 sees the 'Jones Goods' No 103 plodding uphill with the 'Scottish Rambler' special from Princes Pier to Glasgow. In the background can be seen the River Clyde and distant hills. *Author*

Elderslie to Princes Pier (15¾ miles)

Not so much a branch line but the G&SWR route to Greenock. The line was opened on 23 December 1869 to the public under an Act of 1865 by the Greenock & Ayrshire Railway. The line was worked by the G&SWR and merged into that company in 1872. Stations were located at Houston (2 miles), Bridge of Weir (4 miles), Kilmacolm (7¾ miles), Greenock Lynedoch (14¼ miles) and Princes Pier (15¾ miles). The G&SWR was providing 20 trains per weekday including expresses in 1922 in competition with the Caledonian. The regular passenger service was withdrawn by BR on 2 February 1959 back from Greenock Princes Pier to Kilmacolm but boat trains ran until 14 February 1966. The line closed to all traffic from 26 September 1966 back to Kilmacolm. The Glasgow Central to Kilmacolm passenger service was withdrawn by the Scottish Region on 3 January 1983, the line closing back to Elderslie to all traffic on the same date. Kilmacolm to Greenock is earmarked for a walkway of 6½ miles. Kilmacolm station buildings have survived but Princes Pier is now the site of a container berth and ocean terminal.

Lugton East Junction to Ardrossan Montgomerie Pier (15¼ miles)

The Caledonian route to Ardrossan started as the Lanarkshire & Ayrshire Railway, incorporated on 28 July 1884 and opened on 3 September 1888 from Barrmill Junction on the Beith branch to Ardrossan, a distance of 12¼ miles. Montgomerie Pier was opened on 2 June 1890. The Caledonian built its own line from Glasgow via Neilston to join the route at Giffen Junction thus providing an uninterrupted run avoiding the rival G&SWR. The new line was opened throughout on 1 May 1904. The distance from Glasgow Central to Ardrossan via the new route was 31¾, miles which gave the CR boat trains and coal trains direct access to the port. Intermediate stations were located at Giffen (20¼ miles from Glasgow), Auchenmade (22 miles), Kilwinning (26¼ miles), Stevenston (29 miles), Salcoates (30¼ miles) and Ardrossan Town (31½ miles). The CR ran six through trains on weekdays with extras on Saturdays. Suburban trains ran to Neilston as well as boat trains on certain days of the week for the Isle of Man and Irish traffic. Following the 1923 Grouping the LMS had two direct routes from Glasgow to Ardrossan. The LMS put a spur in at Ardeer to enable trains to run off the ex-G&SWR line on to the CR in 1947. Montgomerie Pier was retained for boat trains after the cessation of regular passenger traffic on the main line from 4 July 1932. Montgomerie Pier to Stevenston survived until 6 May 1968, the Giffen to Kilwinning section having closed to all traffic from 30 March 1953. The Giffen to Lugton East section closed to all traffic on 31 May 1950 with the section from Lugton on the main line to Neilston High closing to all traffic from 14 December 1964. The passenger service to Uplawmoor was withdrawn by BR from 2 April 1962. Today, trains run from Neilston to Glasgow as part of the Strathclyde suburban system. The platforms remain at Lugton and Giffen is still in situ.

'B1' class 4-6-0 No 61342 has arrived at Ardrossan Montgomerie Pier with the 1966 'Scottish Rambler' on 10 April 1966. Montgomerie Pier was the Caledonian Railway terminus and was finally closed by the Scottish Region on 5 June 1968. *Author*

Ardrossan Winton Pier with Class 4 2-6-4T No 80047 leaving with the 2.48pm for Glasgow St Enoch on 14 July 1962. The route headcode is displayed on the locomotive buffer beam. *R. Hamilton*

West Kilbride with BR Standard 2-6-0 No 76070 on the 6.33pm Largs to Law Junction on 14 July 1962. In the background under the bridge can be seen the magnificent ex-G&SWR signalbox. *R. Hamilton*

Ardrossan South Beach sees plenty of activity as Standard Class 3 2-6-0 No 77015 arrives with the 1.41pm Kilmarnock to Ardrossan Town. The BR Class 3 2-6-0s consisted of a class of only 20 engines, designed at Swindon and introduced in 1954. No examples have survived into preservation. *R. Hamilton*

Salcoats Central on 14 July 1962 with Class 4 2-6-4T No 42194, built at Derby in 1948, on the 4.20pm Glasgow to Winton Pier. The spruced up engine was one of the Fairburn batch of 2-6-4Ts built by the LMS from 1945, and survived until 1965. *R. Hamilton*

Kilwinning (East) to Irvine Bank Street
(3¼ miles)

The Caledonian provided a branch from Kilwinning to Irvine in competition with the G&SWR main line. The line was opened on 2 June 1890, the same day as Montgomerie Pier under the Lanarkshire & Ayrshire Railway Act of 1884. There was an intermediate halt at Bogside, ½ mile short of Irvine. The station building at Irvine was converted from two villas in Bank Street which were converted into flats by the LMS after closure. The CR provided eight trains on Mondays to Fridays and 10 on Saturdays. The LMS withdrew the passenger service on 28 July 1930 and freight on 1 June 1939. The station building and site were later occupied by a timber company but the whole site has now been cleared.

Giffen to Kilbirnie (4¼ miles)

The Caledonian branch to Kilbirnie was opened on 2 December 1889 for passengers as part of the Lanarkshire & Ayrshire system under the 1884 Act. Intermediate stations were at Brackenhills (1¼ miles) and Glengarnock (2¾ miles). The CR provided nine trains per weekday with two extras on Saturdays. The LMS withdrew the passenger service and the freight from Glengarnock to Giffen on 1 December 1930. With the closure of the steel works at Glengarnock the stub end of the branch to Kilbirnie was closed to all traffic from 19 December 1977, as was the former main line of the G&SWR back to Brownhill Junction. The section from Kilbirnie (G&SWR) to Elderslie Cart Junction (the loop line of 1905) was closed to all traffic on 3 July 1972, the passenger service having been diverted on and from 27 June 1966. None of the stations has survived.

Lugton to Beith (5 miles)

Part of the Glasgow, Barrhead & Kilmarnock Joint, the Beith branch was opened for traffic on 26 June 1873, the same day as the main line to Kilmarnock. An intermediate station was located at Barrmill, three miles from Lugton, and eight trains per weekday were run with two extras on Saturdays. The Caledonian arrived on the scene on 4 September 1888 with the Barrmill & Kilwinning Railway of 1883 which later became the Lanarkshire & Ayrshire Railway, a Caledonian satellite. BR used its four-wheeled railbuses which did nine trips up and down the branch on Mondays to Fridays with two extras on Saturdays. The railbus did not, however, save the branch, which closed to passengers on 5 November 1962 and freight on 5 October 1964. The Giffen to Lugton section via Barrmill is retained for the MoD depot at Giffen. Beith station site is now cleared for housing.

Beith Town with AC Cars railbus No SC79979, a four-wheeled vehicle, which worked the branch from Lugton on the former G&SWR/CR joint line. This view of 29 July 1960 shows the loco shed with a substantial coal stack in the background. *Author*

A good general view of Beith Town on 29 July 1960 with the branch four-wheeled railbus in the platform. The railbus experiment did not last long for BR withdrew the passenger service on 5 November 1962. Freight traffic was withdrawn on 5 October 1964 but part of the branch was retained for MoD traffic to Giffen. *Author*

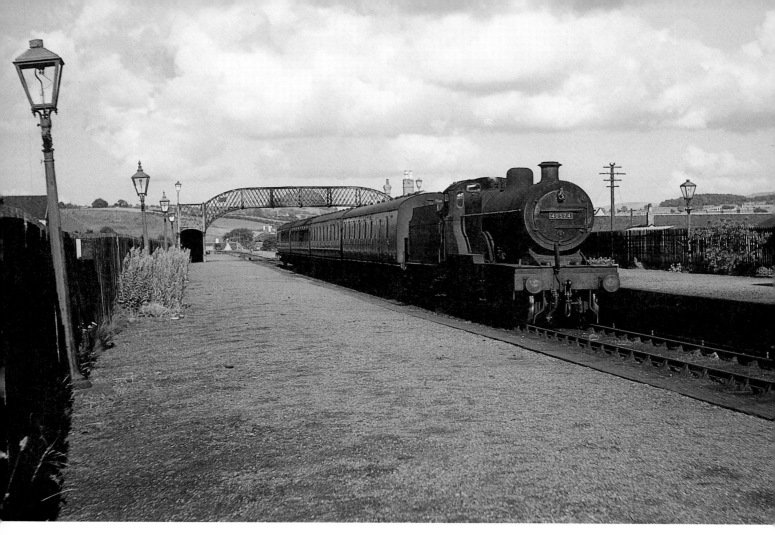

Darvel on 30 July 1960 with LMS '2P' 4-4-0 No 40574 built at Derby in 1928 and withdrawn in 1961. The passenger service to Darvel was withdrawn by BR on 6 April 1964 and little remains to be seen today of the former station. *Author*

Caledonian 0-6-0 No 57579 leaves Darvel with the 5.2pm to Ardrossan on 30 August 1961. The '812' class was built at St Rollox to the design of McIntosh and a member of the class, No 828, has been restored to working order. *R. Hamilton*

Newmilns on the Darvel branch with the AC Cars four-wheeled railbus leaving for Kilmarnock on 19 May 1962. The railbus also did stints on the Lugton to Beith line. The passenger service did not have long to go as BR withdrew it on 6 April 1964. *R. Hamilton*

Hurlford to Darvel (7¼ miles)
Darvel to Strathaven (11 miles)
Hurlford to Galston (3½ miles) was opened on 9 August 1848, extended to Newmilns (5¼ miles) on 20 May 1850 and Darvel (7¼ miles) on 1 June 1896. The G&SWR was providing a service of 11 trains per weekday from Kilmarnock with two extras on Saturdays at the Grouping. An end-on connection with the Caledonian was planned and under an Act of 1896 the CR was to be extended to join up with the G&SWR at Darvel. The CR built their line from Strathaven to County Boundary Junction to join up with the G&SWR, a distance of 6¾ miles. At the boundary, interchange sidings were built and the CR finished the line off for the G&SWR by building the 4¼ miles to Darvel. The through route was opened for goods traffic on 4 July 1904 and each company was to take turns in working the goods

and passenger trains. The passenger working consisted of two trains per weekday, one in the morning and one in the afternoon. This token service from Darvel to Strathaven called at Loudounhill (2¾ miles), Drumclog (5½ miles), Ryeland (7¼ miles) and Strathaven Central (11 miles). The regular passenger service lasted until 1 January 1917 when the rails were lifted to be sent to France. Ryeland reopened to passengers on 1 September 1919 and three trains were provided to Strathaven on weekdays with two extras on Saturdays. The through service recommenced in 1922 and was continued by the LMS until 11 September 1939 when the line was closed to all traffic except for Ryeland Creamery, but the rails were not lifted until 1951. The Darvel passenger service was withdrawn by BR on 6 April 1964 and the freight on 6 July 1964. Little remains to be seen today of the former stations.

Dalry with ex-LMS '2P' 4-4-0 No 40695 heading the 4.20pm St Enoch to Kilmarnock on 29 July 1960. Parcels and mail are being loaded into the front and rear guard's brakes. The line to Kilmarnock was closed to all traffic by BR on 1 October 1973. *Author*

Strathaven Central on 2 September 1961 with a diesel multiple-unit from Hamilton on what was once a through line to Kilmarnock via Darvel which the LMS closed to passengers on 11 September 1939. The Strathaven to Hamilton passenger service was withdrawn by BR on 4 October 1965. *Author*

Crosshouse to Irvine (5½ miles)

The G&SWR had a service from Kilmarnock to Irvine with some trains to Glasgow and others to Ardrossan. Ten trains per weekday used the line with three extras on Saturdays. There were stations at Springside (4 miles from Kilmarnock) and Dreghorn (5¼ miles). The line was opened on 22 May 1848, closed by BR to passengers on 6 April 1964 and freight on 11 October 1965. Kilmarnock to Dalry on the former G&SWR main line was closed to all traffic on 1 October 1973.

Blantyre to Strathaven Central (11¼ miles)

The Hamilton & Strathaven Railway, an independent concern, was authorised on 10 August 1857 to run from Strathaven Junction on the Caley main line north of Hamilton to Strathaven North. The line opened throughout for goods on 1 December 1862 and passengers on 2 February 1863. The Caledonian backed the railway financially and completed the engineering works, finally absorbing the local company on 25 July 1864. The Blantyre to Auchinraith Junction spur was put in on 1 May 1882. The Caledonian Railway provided seven passenger workings on Mondays to Fridays with 13 on Saturdays. There were direct through workings from Glasgow via Blantyre on Saturdays as well as Mondays to Fridays. There were stations at Strathaven North (¾ mile), Glassford (2½ miles), Quarter Road (5 miles), Meikle Earnock (6½ miles) and High Blantyre (9¼ miles). Under the LMS the passenger service had been reduced to four trains per day with the withdrawal taking place on 1 October 1945. Strathaven Central to High Blantyre was closed to freight on 21 September 1953 and High Blantyre to Strathaven Junction on 1 June 1960. Little or no remains of the stations can be seen today.

The 1894-built 'Jones Goods', the first 4-6-0 in Britain, plods through Busby with the 'Scottish Rambler' on 17 April 1965. The Busby Railway opened on 1 January 1866 was extended to East Kilbride on 1 September 1868 and worked by the Caledonian Railway. The line is still open to East Kilbride. *Author*

East Kilbride on 1 September 1961 shows the passenger platform loaded with parcels with a mixed freight being shunted, consisting of open mineral and container wagons. The goods yard is full of empty mineral wagons waiting to be shunted in this truly busy scene. *Author*

Pollockshaws to Hunthill Junction (12¼ miles)

The Busby Railway was authorised on 11 May 1863 and opened on 1 January 1866 from Busby Junction on the Caledonian Neilston line. The railway was extended to East Kilbride on 1 September 1868 and worked by the CR from the outset. The distance from Glasgow was 11½ miles. On 2 July 1885 the line was extended to join up with the Hamilton & Strathaven Railway at Hunthill Junction where a through service of three trains per weekday was provided from Glasgow Central to Hamilton Central, a total distance of 18¼ miles. The CR closed the East Kilbride to Hunthill Junction section during World War 2 and the LMS abolished the passenger service from 14 July 1924. Freight lasted under BR until 24 January 1966, the Hunthill Junction to Mavor & Coulsons Siding section having been withdrawn under LMS ownership from 18 November 1935. There was an intermediate station at Calderwood Glen, 2½ miles from East Kilbride, which is now the terminus of the suburban service from Glasgow. Calderwood Glen was used by excursion trains until 1939.

Hamilton Central to Coalburn (16¾ miles)

The Newton to Hamilton line opened for traffic on 17 September 1849. The line from Motherwell to Coalburn was opened for mineral traffic on 1 December 1856, having been authorised on 24 July 1851. Hamilton (Central) to Strathaven opened to mineral traffic on 1 September 1864 and passengers on 1 December 1866. The Merryton Junction to Stonehouse East, Stonehouse to Blackwood and Alton Heights lines opened on 1 July 1905. The Caledonian provided a passenger service from Hamilton Central to Coalburn of six trains per weekday with an extra on Saturdays. Stations served were Ferniegair (2 miles), Larkhill Central (4¼ miles), Stonehouse (7¼ miles), Blackwood (10½ miles), Lesmahagow (13¾ miles) and Coalburn (16¾ miles). On this passenger service some trains went via Larkhill East (4 miles), Dalserf (5¼ miles), Netherburn (7½ miles), Tillietudlem (8¾ miles) and Blackwood to Coalburn. Auchenheath (10¼ miles) and Brocketsbrae (13 miles) were served by five trains per weekday with one train going through to Coalburn. Thus Coalburn could claim to be served by trains on three different routes from Hamilton Central. Strathaven was also served by five trains via Stonehouse on Mondays to Fridays with two extras on Saturdays.

The mini-system was known as the Lesmahagow Branches, a separate concern but controlled by the Caledonian. The service ran more or less as originally planned under the CR and was perpetuated by the LMS which closed the Dalserf to Stonehouse East section on 7 January 1935. BR withdrew passenger trains from Blackwood Junction and Brocketsbrae to Hamilton on 1 October 1951 and the Hamilton/Strathaven diesel multiple-units on 4 October 1965. All freight had been withdrawn back to Haughead Junction by 4 November 1968. Today, the area is railless beyond the Hamilton to Motherwell circle but there is a plan to extend the existing railway from Hamilton to Larkhill through Merryton using the old trackbed. The Stonehouse-Blackwood-Alton Heights section is earmarked for the Lesmahagow Walkway. The sites at Ferniegair and Larkhall Central stations have been retained for reopening. Blackwood old station is now a house, Lesmahagow has a school on the site and at Coalburn a level crossing gate survives. At Larkhill East the goods shed survives, at Tillietudlem the platforms exist, but the rest of the stations have been demolished. The station house remains at Brocketsbrae.

Coalburn on 2 September 1961 with Caledonian signals and signalbox with the double gates closed to trains. The terminus was closed to passengers on 4 October 1965 and freight shortly afterwards. One of the level crossing gates survives. *Author*

Shettleston to Hamilton (8 miles)

The North British served Hamilton as well as the Caledonian and arrived on the scene to rival the latter company on 1 April 1878 when a passenger service was inaugurated. The Glasgow, Hamilton & Coatbridge Railway was incorporated on 16 July 1874 and was worked by the North British. Stations were located at Mount Vernon (¾ mile), Broomhouse (1¾ miles), Maryville (2½ miles), Uddingston West (3¼ miles), Uddingston (4 miles), Bothwell (5½ miles), Burnbank (6¾ miles), Peacock Cross (7½ miles) and Hamilton (8 miles). Maryville was closed prior to World War 1 and Broomhouse on 24 September 1927. The NBR passenger service ran through from Clydebank and Hyndland on weekdays and was perpetuated by the LNER after 1923. BR withdrew the passenger service on 15 September 1952 from Hamilton back to Bothwell and on to Shettleston on 4 July 1955. Freight had ceased to Shettleston by 4 October 1965 from Bothwell. In 1952, the Hamilton to Bothwell section was closed to all traffic except for the Allanshaw Foundry to Blantyre Junction section which was used until 11 February 1963. The stations have disappeared from the line but platform remains can be seen at Broomhouse and Peacock Cross. A new housing estate covers the site at Burnbank.

The North British Hamilton branch daily goods is seen being shunted by 'N15' class 0-6-2T No 69196, a Reid NBR design of 1910. The station platform is at Peacock Cross and the scene was photographed on 6 November 1961, passenger services having been withdrawn in 1952. *R. Hamilton*

Bothwell NBR station with a Gresley 'V1' 2-6-2T on the last day of passenger operation. The service was withdrawn by the Scottish Region of BR on and from 10 July 1955. The Gresley 'V1/V3' 2-6-2Ts were extinct by the end of 1964 and no examples have survived. *W. S. Sellar*

Fallside to Bothwell (1¼ miles)

The Caledonian had a short branch off the main line at Fallside and ran a through service to Glasgow Central of 12 trains per weekday with extras on Saturdays. The branch was closed to all traffic on 5 June 1950. A factory now covers the site of the old station at Bothwell.

Coatbridge to Bothwell (6¼ miles)

Opened on 1 April 1878 as part of the GH&CR scheme, the NBR service was from Clydebank or Hyndland via Coatbridge to Hamilton. There were stations at Coatbridge Central (½ mile), Whifflet (1¼ miles) and Bellshill (3½ miles) of which there is now no trace. Trains ran on weekdays only and the LNER closed Whifflet station on 22 September 1930. The LNER used one of its steam Sentinel railcars, No 37 Clydesdale, on the branch in prewar days. BR withdrew the passenger service from Bothwell via Coatbridge and Blairhill on 10 September 1951. Whifflet East Junction to Bothwell closed to all traffic on 10 July 1955. On the NBR line north of Coatbridge, originally opened in 1826 as the Monkland & Kirkintilloch Railway, the section from Bedlay to Lenzie (Garngaber Junction) was closed to all traffic on 28 February 1966. Bedlay Colliery to Garnqueen closed to all traffic after 10 June 1981. Part of the Bothwell to Uddingston section is now a footpath.

Holytown to Morningside (6 miles)

The Wishaw & Coltness Railway opened to Holytown from Whifflet on 23 January 1834 with Newarthill (later Carfin) being reached by the W&CR on 31 May 1834. Morningside opened to passengers on 9 March 1844 with trains via Motherwell. The direct line through Cleland and Newmains was opened by the W&CR under an Act of 16 July 1846. The Caledonian ran a weekday service of five trains with an extra on Saturdays (1922 *Bradshaw*) and the LMS withdrew the passenger service on 1 December 1930. There were two intermediate stations on the line, at Cleland (2½ miles), and Newmains (4 miles). The LMS continued to use the line for freight traffic until 20 May 1939 and lifted the Cleland Junction to Newmains section in 1941. Newmains back to Morningside closed on 5 February 1951 to freight and the stations have now been demolished.

Airdrie to Newhouse (3¾ miles)
Airdrie to Langloan (3 miles)

The Caledonian opened its line to Airdrie on 1 June 1886 from Coatbridge and extended to Newhouse on 2 July 1888. The station at Airdrie was a dead-end terminal with the Caledonian providing a passenger service of eight trains per weekday with four extras on Saturdays. Stations were built at Calderbank (1½ miles), Chapelhall (2½ miles) and Newhouse (3¾ miles). The CR provided 13 trains per weekday on Mondays to Fridays with three extras on Saturdays from Maryhill to Airdrie via Coatbridge. The Caley also worked a Coatbridge to Glenboig service of 10 passenger trains per weekday with two extras on Saturdays. The Glenboig trains worked over NBR tracks from Gartsherrie to Garnqueen South Junction. Gartsherrie station closed on 28 October 1940 and Glenboig on 11 June 1956. The LMS withdrew the Airdrie to Newhouse trains on 1 December 1930 and Airdrie to Whifflet Upper service on 3 May 1943. BR withdrew

freight from Airdrie to Calder on 6 July 1964. With the decline in the coal traffic BR closed the Chapelhall to Bellside Junction (Cleland) section on 4 April 1966, the Salsburgh mineral branches having closed back to Lanridge Junction on 2 March 1964. Airdrie (CR) station site is now a supermarket and bus station but the platform remains at Whifflet Upper.

Coatbridge to Manuel (17½ miles)
Blackston to Bathgate (4 miles)

The North British ran a passenger service from Blairhill to Manuel and Bathgate via Coatbridge, Sunnyside and Blackston. The railways to the north of Airdrie had got off to an early start with the Monkland & Kirkintilloch opened in 1826 as a horse-worked concern to take coal from the Monklands down to the Forth & Clyde Canal. The Ballochney Railway followed with a system to join up with the M&KR in 1828 and was later joined with the Slamannan in 1840. The Slamannan Railway was opened from Airdriehill to Causewayend where it joined up with the Union Canal on 5 August 1840. Passengers were conveyed by train to Causewayend and canal to Edinburgh until the coming of the Edinburgh & Glasgow Railway. A passenger service was started on 26 December 1844 from Airdrie to Glasgow Queen Street. The M&K, Ballochney and Slamannan companies got together and under an Act of 14 August 1848 amalgamated to form the Monkland Railways Co. The railways were built to a 4ft 6in gauge originally and this was converted to standard in 1847. The Monkland Railways eventually became part of the North British empire. The passenger service to Causewayend was sparse, stations being situated at Commonhead (1¾ miles), Rawyards (2¼ miles), Whiterigg (3½ miles), Longriggend (6½ miles), Slamannan (9¼ miles), Avonbridge (12¾ miles), Blackston (13¼ miles), Bowhouse (15½ miles), Causewayend (16½ miles) and Manuel (17½ miles). The weekdays only service consisted of three trains per Monday to Friday with an extra on Saturdays to Bathgate and two through trains to Manuel from Blairhill. There were also two Bathgate to Manuel trains via Blackston. On the Bathgate line (opened 1856) there was an intermediate station at Westfield, 1¼ miles from Blackston. The LNER as inheritor of the system withdrew the passenger service from Blackston to Bathgate Upper and Manuel (LL) to Coatbridge Greenside Junction on 5 May 1930. The once extensive Ballochney system was closed down as the pits closed, the last piece of the Monklands ceased to function after the closure of the Commonhead to Kipps Incline Foot section on 6 July 1964 and Kipps Incline Foot to Greenside Junction on 18 August 1971. Westfield station house and viaduct survive and an official walk now runs from Greenside Junction near Coatbridge through Airdrie to Whiterigg where the platforms survive. The section through Commonhead and Rawyards has been landscaped and built upon. Slamannan has disappeared and Avonbridge has been built over. Part of one of the platforms at Blackston has survived but Bathgate Lower has been built over. The rest of the stations have gone but there is a trace of Manuel Low Level.

Airdrie to Bathgate (14½ miles)

The North British ran an alternative service from Edinburgh to Glasgow via Bathgate which was introduced on 1 April 1871. The line had opened to Bathgate on 12 November 1849 and Airdrie on 11 August 1862. Stations were built at Clarkston (1½ miles), Plains (2½ miles), Caldercruix (4½ miles), Forrestfield (6 miles), Westcraigs (9¼ miles) and Armadale (12 miles). The NBR ran five through trains from Edinburgh on weekdays, two of which ran fast from Bathgate to Airdrie. Four trains started from Bathgate and four from Caldercruix at the time of the Grouping. The LNER watered down the service prior to Nationalisation and only ran one through train from Edinburgh and two from Bathgate. BR withdrew the passenger service on 9 January 1956 but kept

the line in use for summer Saturday trains until 1960. The route was not abandoned until 1 February 1982 when the Bathgate to Plains section was closed. Trains now run through to Helensburgh Central from Drumgelloch and Airdrie every half an hour every day of the week. The line east of Drumgelloch is today being developed by Sustrans as a public footpath and cycleway. The station sites have been landscaped and little has survived except for the platform edges at some of the stations. The station houses survive at Westcraigs and Forrestfield.

The locomotive poses by the side of Castlehill Junction signalbox with the engine crew holding the nameplate up for the photographer. The NBR signalman's steps can be seen between the loco and the signalbox. The LNER withdrew the passenger service from Morningside to Bathgate on 1 May 1930. *W. S. Sellar*

Morningside to Bathgate Upper (14 miles)

The North British opened its Morningside to Bathgate line on 1 October 1864, with intermediate stations at Fauldhouse (7½ miles), Bents (9½ miles) and Whitburn (11¾ miles). The passenger service consisted of five trains per weekday with an extra on Saturdays. The LNER withdrew the passenger trains on 1 May 1930 but freight lasted longer. The Blackhall Junction to Shotts mineral line closed on 6 March 1950 and the Shotts to Westcraigs Junction lines on 17 June 1963. The

Carluke goods branch closed to all traffic back to Castlehill Branch Junction on 4 April 1949. Kingshill Colliery to Morningside via Castle Hill Branch Junction was closed back from Kingshill Colliery on 15 July 1974. The Whitburn to Addiewell NB line closed on 24 April 1963 and the Bathgate-Fauldhouse section on 10 August 1964, both to all traffic. The sites of the two Morningside stations have been cleared and no buildings have survived. The line can be walked as far as Kingshill Colliery but after that the old line has been obliterated by opencast working.

Lanark with Caledonian 0-6-0 No 57618 on 2 September 1961 with the Muirkirk train. The Caley '812' class 0-6-0s were classified '3F' by the LMS and only one example has survived. *Author*

Lanark to Muirkirk (18¾ miles)

The Lanark Railway opened from Cleghorn on the Caledonian main line on 5 January 1855 and was acquired by the CR on 23 July 1860. An extension onward to Douglas was opened on 1 April 1864 and continued to Muirkirk on 1 June 1874 where a connection was made with the G&SWR branch from Auchinleck. A through passenger service from Ayr to Edinburgh via this route was tried in 1878 but was not a success. The Muirkirk branch was joined up with the Lesmahagow lines by the Muirkirk & Lesmahagow Junction Railway on 2 April 1883 from Poneil Junction to Alton Heights Junction. Regular passenger traffic was scarce on this line but it was a very useful freight link. The Caledonian opened stations at Sandilands (7¼ miles from Lanark), Ponfeigh (9 miles), Douglas (11 miles), Douglas West (14¼ miles), Inches (17¼ miles), Glenbuck (19¾ miles) and Muirkirk (23½ miles). The passenger service consisted of four trains per weekday with an extra on Mondays (1922

Bradshaw). There was an unusual service to Brocketsbrae of one train from Lanark and two return workings with two of the trains originating and returning to Hamilton. The four trains per day passenger service ran through the LMS years and survived until the advent of BR but there were six trains on Saturdays and a Wednesdays only working to Douglas West. Glenbuck was closed to passengers on 4 August 1952 and Douglas was renamed to Happendon by the LMS. The regular passenger working over the Poneil Junction to the Brocketsbrae line was withdrawn on 11 September 1939 but freight lasted until 13 September 1954. BR withdrew the passenger service from Muirkirk to Lanark on 5 October 1964 which included closure to all traffic from Muirkirk to Ponfeigh. Ponfeigh to Lanark lasted until 15 January 1968 for freight traffic. Lanark today survives with an hourly service to Glasgow on weekdays. Little remains of the stations on the branch today as they have all been demolished.

Lanark on 16 October 1965 with a BLS railtour headed by the GNSR 4-4-0, *Gordon Highlander*. The line to Muirkirk was closed to passengers on 5 October 1964 but Lanark is now part of the suburban system with an hourly service. *Author*

Muirkirk with Caley 0-6-0 No 57295 ready to depart for Lanark with the fireman bringing the headlamp up to place above the smokebox handrail. The engine dated from 1887, having been built at the CR workshops at St Rollox. *Author*

Muirkirk to Auchinleck (10¼ miles)

The G&SWR opened its branch to Muirkirk on 9 August 1848 from Auchinleck, the line having been authorised under the Glasgow, Dumfries & Carlisle Act of 1846. The end-on junction with the Caledonian was made after that company had completed the line from Douglas in 1874. The G&SWR provided four trains per weekday with an extra on Saturdays to Auchinleck and three to Ayr with an extra on Saturdays. Stations were at Cronberry (6½ miles), Lugar (7½ miles) and Commondyke (8¼ miles). The LMS perpetuated the basic service but BR wielded the axe and withdrew the passenger trains on 3 July 1950. The NCB branch to Lugar Ironworks was closed to all traffic on 23 February 1970 and the Cronberry to Auchinleck section closed to freight on 6 December 1976. A proposed new pit at Cronberry (Powharnel) would mean the reopening of the line back to Auchinleck on the main line but plans have yet to be implemented. Muirkirk G&SWR station building is still in situ.

Muirkirk to Ayr (26 miles)

A service to Ayr was provided by the G&SWR via Cronberry and Annbank Junction. Passenger traffic commenced from Cronberry through to Annbank on 1 July 1872. At Annbank the line joined up with the Mauchline to Ayr section, opened to all traffic on 1 September 1870. A connection with the Dalmellington branch from Belston Junction to Holehouse was completed in the same year. The G&SWR ran a through service from Muirkirk to Ayr of three trains per weekday with an extra on Saturdays. Coal traffic was more lucrative than the passenger service and lasted well into BR days. Stations were located at Cumnock (9¾ miles), Dumfries House (11¼ miles), Skares (12¼ miles), Ochiltree (13¾ miles), Drongan (16 miles), Trabboch (20 miles), Annbank (22¾ miles) and Auchincruive (24¼ miles). The LMS reduced the passenger service to two trains per weekday with an extra on Saturdays prior to 1948 with BR withdrawing the service on 10 September 1951. The coal traffic lasted longer and the NCB opened a new pit at Killoch near Ochiltree in 1959. Muirkirk to Cronberry Junction closed to freight on 10 February 1969, Cronberry to Dykes Junction on 7 March 1964 and Dykes Junction to Belston Junction on 3 April 1966. The Killoch Washery to Annbank section is still in situ. The Ayr to Mauchline section had a passenger service following the closure of the Dumfries to Stranraer route but closed again from 5 May 1975. The G&SWR line from Monkton, opened in 1892, was severed when the Glenburn to Mossblown Junction section closed on 15 November 1949. Today not much remains of the line but part of the route is walkable.

A quiet moment at Catrine, the terminus of the former G&SWR branch from Brackenhill Junction. The garden on the platform has been carefully tended in this scene photographed in the summer before closure. The station has been demolished and the site is now derelict. *Lens of Sutton*

Class 4 2-6-4T No 42277 leaves Catrine on an SLS/RCTS railtour on 20 June 1962. The branch was closed to passengers on 3 May 1943 and to all traffic from 6 July 1964. *R. Hamilton*

Mauchline to Catrine (3½ miles)

The line from Brackenhill Junction to Catrine opened for traffic on 1 March 1903, the distance from the main line to Catrine being a mere 1 mile 35 chains. The G&SWR provided seven passenger trains on Mondays to Fridays with four extras on Saturdays. The line was closed in 1916 and when reopened had a service of three Monday to Friday trains with a Saturday extra. The LMS perpetuated this reduced service which was withdrawn on 3 May 1943. The line was visited by an RCTS/SLS special on 20 June 1962 prior to closure to all traffic by BR on 6 July 1964. The station at Catrine has been demolished and the site is now a car park.

Dalmellington during the heyday of the Class 2P 4-4-0s with No 40595 of 1928 with an Ayr train on 9 May 1959. The engine only had two years to go and was withdrawn in 1961. The branch closed to passengers on 6 April 1964.
E. Wilmshurst

Ayr to Dalmellington (15 miles)
Holehouse to Rankinston (4¾ miles)

The Ayr & Dalmellington Railway opened for passengers on 7 August 1856 under an Act of 1853. The A&DR had its own terminus at Ayr Townhead but trains ran through to the G&SWR station. The G&SWR absorbed the A&DR in 1858 which had been used by the Ayr & Maybole Railway as far as Dalrymple Junction, three miles from Ayr, from 13 October 1856. The A&MR became part of the G&SWR system from 29 June 1871. The Dalmellington section became a branch of what was later to become the main line to Stranraer. From 1872 a connecting line was opened from the Dalmellington branch to Belston Junction on the Muirkirk to Ayr line opened in the same year. Passenger services were not introduced until 1 January 1884 when an intermediate station was opened at Rankinston. The old A&DR station at Ayr was replaced in 1886. Passenger services from Rankinston were meagre, there being only three trains per weekday, one of which went via Annbank, but there was an additional train on Tuesdays and Saturdays. The stations on the Dalmellington branch were located at Hollybush (6¼ miles from Ayr), Patna (9¾ miles) and Waterside (11¾ miles). Seven trains per weekday were run from Ayr by the G&SWR and five by the LMS which put on extras on Saturdays. BR withdrew the Rankinston trains on 3 April 1950 and closed the line to all traffic to Holehouse Junction. Littlemill Colliery back to Belston Junction lasted until 1 January 1975. Under the Scottish Region four-wheeled railbuses were introduced but this did not save the line which closed to passengers on 6 April 1964 and freight back to Waterside on 6 July 1964. Today, Waterside is still served by rail for the Chalmerston Scottish Coal sidings where there is a connection with the Ayrshire Railway Preservation Society at Dunaskin. The ARPS has now commenced a service and Waterside station is being renovated. Hollybush station house remains in use.

Dalmellington on 30 July 1960 with four-wheel Park Royal railbus unloading. The railbuses were a brief experiment on the Region and did not survive, mainly because the branch lines that they served closed. *Author*

The branch to Heads of Ayr was worked on summer Saturdays by an assortment of motive power including '4F' 0-6-0s. A member of this ubiquitous class is about to pull out of Ayr on 30 July 1960. The line closed on 16 September 1968. *Author*

Heads of Ayr was the terminus of the line from Ayr when this picture was taken on 30 July 1960. Passengers had direct access to the nearby Butlins camp until the line was closed in September 1968. Heads of Ayr to Girvan closed to all traffic on 28 February 1955. *Author*

Ayr to Girvan (21¾ miles)

The main line to Girvan was opened on 24 May 1860 by the Maybole & Girvan Railway under an Act of 14 July 1856. The M&GR was amalgamated into the G&SWR on 5 July 1865 and later extended southwards to Challoch Junction on 5 October 1870. The coastal line from Ayr to Girvan via Alloway Junction was opened on 17 May 1906 as a light railway. The G&SWR built a hotel and golf course at Turnberry and supplied a railway to serve the tourists. The Maidens & Dunure Light Railway was opened under the 1896 Light Railways Act and was wholly owned by the G&SWR. Stations were located at Alloway (3 miles from Ayr), Heads of Ayr (6¼ miles), Dunure (8 miles), Knoweside (11 miles), Glenside (13 miles), Maidens (15¼ miles) and Turnberry (16¾ miles). Eight trains were run on weekdays including a breakfast car express at 7.25am from Girvan and an afternoon tea car from Glasgow. The passenger service was withdrawn from Alloway Junction to Turnberry on 1 December 1930, restarted in 1932 and withdrawn again in June 1933. Turnberry to Girvan closed to passengers on 2 March 1942 but the Heads of Ayr to Alloway Junction section reopened on 17 May 1947 for Butlin's to which special trains were run in the summer. BR finally withdrew the Heads of Ayr trains on 16 September 1968 when the line closed to all traffic. The summer timetable for 1960 shows business to be brisk with six trains on weekdays and 10 on Saturdays. The section below Heads of Ayr to Girvan had ceased to be used after the withdrawal of freight trains on 28 February 1955. Heads of Ayr, Knoweside, Glenside and Maidens are now caravan sites. Turnberry is now part of the hotel complex and adjacent golf course.

Kilmarnock to Troon (9 miles)

Not so much a branch line but an early inter-city and Scotland's first railway, authorised on 27 May 1808. The line was double-tracked and laid to a 4ft gauge. The K&T was opened for business on 6 July 1812. Steam locomotives were tried in 1816 but were not a success so the railway reverted to horses which worked until 1847. The Glasgow, Paisley, Kilmarnock & Ayr Railway took over in 1846 and eventually, in 1899, the line became part of the G&SWR system. The railway was modified in 1845 and 1865 and is still in use as part of the present network. A connecting line from Gatehead to the Darvel line was opened on 14 July 1902 and a passenger station built at Riccarton which was never used for regular traffic. Freight traffic lasted until 31 March 1971 from Riccarton to Kay Park Junction, serving the power station at Craigie. The line was visited on 16 April 1965 by the 'Scottish Rambler' railtour.

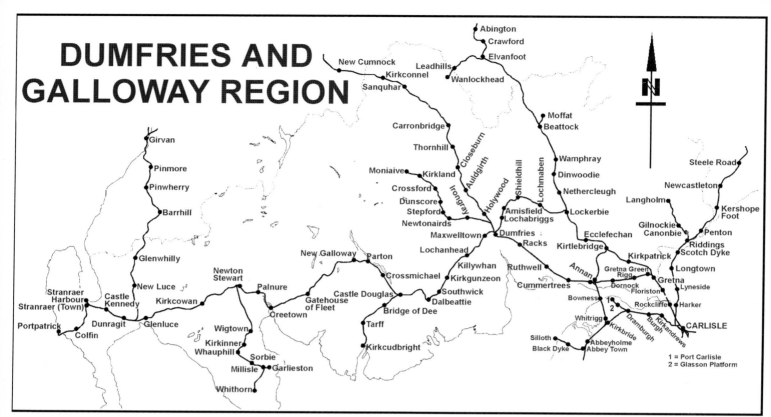

DUMFRIES AND GALLOWAY REGION

Moffat station on the last day with Caley 0-4-4T No 55232 and a single coach which the engine propelled along the branch to Beattock. The line was closed to passenger traffic on 6 December 1954 and freight trains were withdrawn on 6 April 1964. *W. A. C. Smith*

Dumfries & Galloway

Elvanfoot to Wanlockhead (7¼ miles)

The Leadhills & Wanlockhead Railway was opened as a light railway under the 1896 Act and was owned by the Caledonian Railway. The first section opened from Elvanfoot to Leadhills on 1 October 1901 followed by Leadhills to Wanlockhead on 12 October 1902. Leadhills was 5¾ miles from Elvanfoot on the Caley main line. At an altitude of 1,413ft above sea level the terminus was the highest point reached by a standard gauge railway in the British Isles. The Caledonian ran three trains per weekday and used specialised rolling stock for the line's operation. The CR used its Drummond 0-4-4 tanks to work the line and four-wheeled coaches with lower step boards enabling passengers to join from the trackside. An unusual feature of the railway was that the stations did not have platforms and passengers could join the train at intermediate locations by hailing it just like a bus! This gem of a railway was closed by the LMS on and from 2 January 1939. Part of the branch has now reopened in Strathclyde as the new Leadhills & Wanlockhead but to a 2ft gauge. The narrow gauge line runs to Hillhead summit 1,498ft above sea level and the owners hope to reopen the line to Wanlockhead at a later date.

Beattock to Moffat (2 miles)

The Moffat Railway was promoted locally to serve the spa town and was authorised in 1881. The line opened to passengers on 2 April 1883 with the Caledonian Railway providing 13 trains on weekdays. The LMS perpetuated the service which, in its later days, was worked by a Caledonian 0-4-4T which propelled one way with the single-coach train. BR withdrew the passenger service on 6 December 1954 and the freight on 6 April 1964. A small platform building remains on site.

Moffat in 1965, a year after final closure, shows the track still in situ but the station building has been removed. The small building at the end of the platform has survived. *Author*

A fine spring day at Shieldhill on the Lockerbie to Dumfries branch with 'Jubilee' class 4-6-0 No 45588 *Kashmir* working the 'Scottish Rambler' special to Stranraer on 15 April 1963. The station building has now been replaced by a house, the line having been closed to all traffic on 18 April 1966. *Author*

Dumfries with ex-Caley 0-6-0 No 57661 shunting container wagons on the Caledonian branch from Lockerbie on 15 April 1963. The engine is a Pickersgill 0-6-0 of 1918 classified '3F' by the LMS and BR. *Author*

Dumfries to Lockerbie (14¾ miles)

The Dumfries, Lochmaben & Lockerbie Railway was authorised on 14 June 1860 and opened on 1 September 1863. The line was worked from the outset by the Caledonian and absorbed on 5 July 1865. The CR ran four trains per weekday with an extra on Saturdays and provided stations at Locharbriggs (2¾ miles), Amisfield (4¼ miles), Shieldhill (7 miles) and Lochmaben (10½ miles). The LMS service was similar at Nationalisation and BR closed the line to passengers on 19 May 1952. Freight traffic lasted longer and ceased after 18 April 1966. Little remains to be seen of the stations nowadays as they have been built over. Parts of the former railway's embankments and cuttings can be see along the course of the line.

Caley '3F' No 57602 shunts vans at Dumfries on 30 July 1960 in the bay platform used for the local trains for Kirkcudbright. The platforms are loaded with parcels traffic, once a common sight on British stations. *Author*

Kirtlebridge to Brayton (21¼ miles)

The Solway Junction Railway was authorised on 30 June 1864 and opened on 13 September 1869 for goods and mineral traffic. The line was a subsidiary of the Caledonian who had running powers over the North British Silloth branch from Kirkbride to Abbeytown Junction. The railway passed over the Solway viaduct, 1,940yd long and built with a single track. The CR built the line to convey iron ore from Cumbria to the ironworks and furnaces of Lanarkshire. The viaduct was found to be unsafe and closed on 1 September 1921 but repairs were not implemented and the LMS as inheritor of the CR dismantled it in 1933. A sparse passenger service was provided by the CR which ran three passenger trains per weekday from Brayton to Annan and six from Annan to Kirtlebridge. The LMS ran the Annan to Kirtlebridge passenger service of four trains per weekday until 27 April 1931. The Brayton to Abbeytown Junction section was closed to freight traffic by the LMS in 1933. The stub end of the Kirtlebridge to Annan section from Annan (CR) was in use by BR until 28 February 1955 from Annan Shawhill to the G&SWR main line. The station buildings remain at Annan and Bowness.

The bridge over the Solway was opened on 13 September 1869 by the Solway Junction Railway and carried mineral traffic for the Caledonian Railway. The viaduct was found to be unsafe and was closed in 1921 and demolished by the LMS in 1933. The CR provided three passenger trains per weekday between Brayton and Annan until closure. *LGRP*

Dumfries to Moniaive (17½ miles)

The Cairn Valley Light Railway was opened for business on 1 March 1905 and worked by the G&SWR using their steam railmotors. The G&SWR provided three trains per weekday but the LMS reduced the service to two trains with an extra on Saturdays. The branch left the main line at Cairn Valley Junction (1¾ miles from Dumfries) and stopped at Irongray (5 miles from Dumfries), Newtonairds (7½ miles), Stepford (8¾ miles), Dunscore (10¾ miles), Crossford (13¾ miles), Kirkland (15¼ miles) and Moniaive (17½ miles). The station at Moniaive was constructed in timber and the single platform with bay had timber edges. The ballast was ash and the rails secondhand from other parts of the system. The railway was lightly laid with few heavy earthworks but there was a viaduct at Dunscore. The ruling gradient was 1 in 65 and the station buildings very moderate. The line was worked on the 'one-engine-in-steam' principle, thus disposing of signalling beyond Cairn Valley Junction. The quarry at Stepford kept the line in business until BR closed the branch to all traffic on 4 July 1949, the passenger service having been withdrawn by the LMS on 3 May 1943. Little remains to be seen of the line today but Crossford station building is now a house.

The rise and decline of a light railway station with a view of Moniaive in passenger days under the LMS and a photograph taken in 1965. The station building has survived in the 1965 view, the passenger service having been withdrawn by the LMS on 3 May 1943. Freight traffic was withdrawn by BR on 4 July 1949. *Lens of Sutton/Author*

The heyday of the light railway shows Dunscore and Irongray stations on the former light railway to Moniaive, opened as the Cairn Valley Light Railway on 1 March 1905. The line was worked by the G&SWR from the opening using steam railcars. Passengers wait at Dunscore for one of the two trains per day. At Irongray the small country station is in an immaculate condition. *Lens of Sutton*

Castle Douglas to Kirkcudbright
(10¼ miles)

The branch to Kirkcudbright was opened to all traffic on 15 August 1864 under the Kirkcudbright Railway Act of 1 August 1861. The railway was worked by the G&SWR and merged into that concern in August 1865. At the Grouping the passenger service consisted of seven trains per weekday with an extra on Saturdays. BR reduced the passenger trains to four on weekdays with an extra on Saturdays. There were two intermediate stations on the line, at Bridge of Dee (2¾ miles from Castle Douglas) and Tarff (6¾ miles). Bridge of Dee station was closed on 26 September 1949 and the rest of the branch on 3 May 1965 to passengers. Freight traffic ceased from 14 June 1965 when the line closed to all traffic. Bridge of Dee and Kirkcudbright stations are now in use as houses but Tarff is derelict.

Tarff was one of the intermediate stations on the Kirkcudbright branch, the other station being Bridge of Dee which was closed on 26 September 1949. The passenger service on the branch was withdrawn by the Scottish Region on 3 May 1965. *Author*

Kirkcudbright station on 30 July 1960 with Class 3 2-6-2T No 40152 about to depart on a Dumfries train. The branch was closed to all traffic on 14 June 1965. The station building is now in use as a house. *Author*

Newton Stewart to Whithorn (19¼ miles)
Millisle to Garlieston (1 mile)

The Wigtownshire Railway was promoted under an Act of 1872 and opened for traffic on 2 August 1875 to Millisle. The Garlieston branch opened on the same day for goods only but financial problems beset the railway and it was not completed until 9 July 1877 through to Whithorn. The Garlieston branch of just over one mile did not have a regular passenger service but excursions used it for the Isle of Man. The Wigtownshire Railway and the Portpatrick Railway amalgamated in 1885 and became the Portpatrick & Wigtownshire Joint which was owned jointly by the LNWR,

Midland, G&SWR and Caledonian. The Whithorn passenger service consisted of four trains per day with an extra on Fridays. The passenger service survived until 25 September 1950 but freight continued until 5 October 1964. The freight worked on Mondays, Wednesdays and Fridays and visited Garlieston on an as-required basis. The stations were located at Wigtown (7 miles), Kirkinner (9½ miles), Whauphill (11 miles), Sorbie (13½ miles), Millisle (15¼ miles) and Whithorn (19¼ miles). The Garlieston branch left the 'main line' at Millisle which is now a house. Sorbie is a house and a fire station has been built at Whithorn; the rest of the stations have been demolished.

Above:
The Whithorn goods stops at Whauphill briefly in August 1960 headed by 'Jumbo' No 57340 built at St Rollox in 1892. All of the 'Jumbos' had been withdrawn by the end of 1963. The station has since been demolished. *Author*

Above right:
Millisle Junction on 30 May 1965, a few months after closure of the Whithorn branch. The rails have been removed and the sleepers will be recovered by the contractor but the buildings have survived as a house. *Author*

Right:
A rare branch was the 1-mile line from Millisle to Garlieston which never had a regular passenger service. The Whithorn goods took freight traffic as required until October 1964. *Author*

Whithorn sees the engine of the three times a week goods running round the train to do a spot of shunting in August 1960. The branch closed to regular passenger services on 25 September 1950 and freight on 5 October 1964. A fire station has since been built on the site of the old station. *Author*

Portpatrick station in LMS days with 'Jumbo' class 0-6-0 No 17440, built at St Rollox in 1896, which has run round the two-coach train ready to return to Stranraer. The line closed to all traffic on 6 February 1950 and the station is now in a caravan site. *Lens of Sutton*

Stranraer to Portpatrick (8¾ miles)

The Portpatrick Railway was authorised in 1857 and opened to Portpatrick Town on 28 August 1862. The harbour branch did not open until 1863 and lasted until 1870. Stranraer Harbour opened on 1 October 1862 and proved to be a far more satisfactory place than the exposed position at Portpatrick. The passenger and freight services lasted until 6 February 1950 when the line was closed to all traffic. There were only two passenger trains per day in the final timetable which was a reduction on the pre-Grouping service of three each way per weekday with an extra market-day working on Fridays. There was an intermediate station at Colfin, 3¼ miles from Portpatrick, and a station at Stranraer Town (7½ miles). Portpatrick is now in use as a caravan site. Colfin station has been incorporated into a creamery and Stranraer Town is still in situ.

No 43011, an Ivatt 2-6-0 of 1948, stands in the platform at Langholm on 10 October 1963 with a two-coach passenger train of LMS stock. The branch was closed to passengers on 15 June 1964 and freight on 18 September 1967, the same year as the locomotive's withdrawal. The site is now a housing estate. *Hugh Ballantyne*

Riddings Junction to Langholm (7 miles)

The Waverley route from Carlisle to Edinburgh was completed on 1 July 1862. The Langholm branch followed and was opened throughout on 18 April 1864 under an Act of 21 July 1859. The North British ran seven trains per weekday on the branch which were reduced to four with an extra on Saturdays by BR. There were intermediate stations at Canonbie (1¼ miles) and Gilnockie (2¾ miles). The passenger service was worked by 'J39' class 0-6-0s in the final years and a through train to Carlisle was run up until closure. BR withdrew the passenger service on 15 June 1964 and freight on 18 September 1967. The terminus site is now occupied by a housing estate.

Ivatt 2-6-0 No 43139 waits at Langholm on 21 October 1961 with the old engine shed to the right which had become redundant by 1961. The branch closed to passengers in 1964 and the station site has since been built over. *A. Moyes*

Longtown to Gretna (Cumbria) (3¼ miles)

The North British had its own line to Gretna from Longtown which was opened in 1861. The NBR ran two passenger trains per weekday through to Gretna Green on the G&SWR main line. The NBR also had its own station at Gretna alongside the Caledonian main line station. The passenger service was discontinued on 7 August 1915 but freight trains used the link until 9 August 1960. Gretna NB station has since disappeared.

Borders

Riccarton Junction to Hexham (42 miles)

A North British incursion into England, the Border Counties Railway passed through remote countryside in Northumbria. The Border Counties opened throughout on 1 July 1862 and was a subsidiary company worked by the NBR which ran trains from Hawick through to Newcastle via Riccarton Junction — a railway settlement with no road access. The NBR provided three trains per weekday at the Grouping, one of which was a Newcastle to Edinburgh service. The three-train service was maintained by the LNER and the line survived until 15 October 1956 for regular passenger traffic. Freight trains ran a little longer and were withdrawn by BR on 1 September 1958 to Hexham with the Bellingham-Reedsmouth-Morpeth section being closed to freight on 11 November 1963. The last passenger train was a ramblers' special from Newcastle to Hawick on 7 September 1958 which ran via Morpeth and Reedsmouth. One of the stations — Saughtree (2¾ miles from Riccarton Junction) — was in Scotland and one — Deadwater (5¾ miles) — just over the border; both are now private residences.

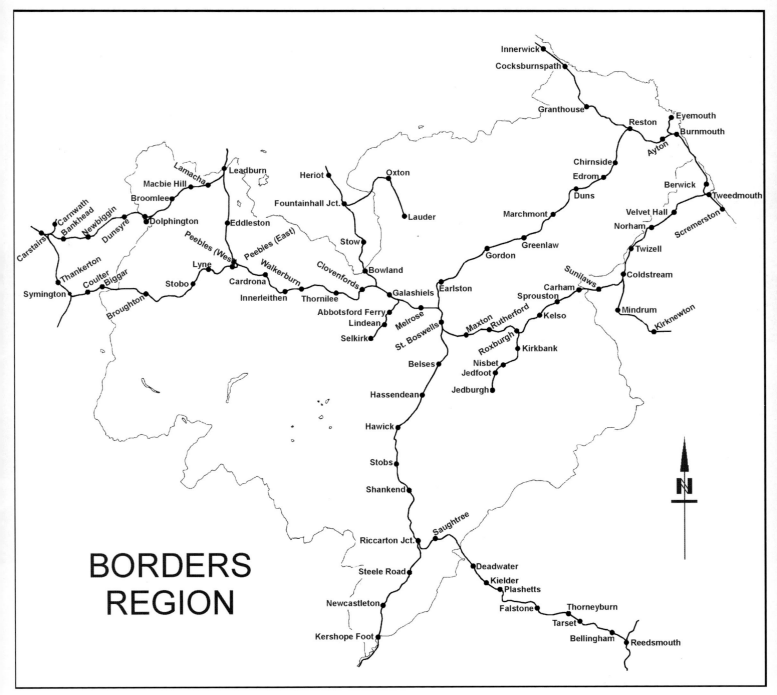

BORDERS REGION

NBR branch lines were worked by Reid 4-4-0s of the 'J' class reclassified 'D30' by the LNER after 1923. A total of 27 engines were built at Cowlairs from 1912 to 1920 and were named after characters in the Scott novels. No 62440 *Wandering Willie* is seen at Hawick on 7 September 1958, having been withdrawn in July. The class was extinct by 1960. *Author*

Jedburgh on the occasion of a visit by the 'Scottish Rambler' on 14 April 1963. The train is seen leaving behind 'B1' class 4-6-0 No 61324 hauling a BR maroon set of standard coaches. The branch closed to freight traffic on and from 10 August 1964, having closed to passengers on 12 August 1948. *Author*

Roxburgh to Jedburgh (7 miles)

The Jedburgh Railway was opened on 17 July 1856 under an Act of 25 May 1855 and was worked by the NBR from the outset, being absorbed on 3 July 1860. Stations were located at Old Ormiston (Kirkbank 1¾ miles), Nisbet (4¼ miles), Jedfoot (5½ miles) and Jedburgh (7 miles). The NBR provided six trains per weekday and two on Sundays which connected at Roxburgh with the St Boswells trains which connected in turn with the East Coast main line. The Sunday service did not survive the 1923 Grouping but trains ran through to Kelso under the LNER. Disaster struck on 12 August 1948 when floods destroyed bridges and permanent way. The passenger service was withdrawn from that date but freight survived until 10 August 1964. The branch was visited by the BLS/SLS 'Scottish Rambler' on 14 April 1963. Jedburgh station was half a mile from the town, where the site has now been built over.

St Boswells to Kelso (11½ miles)

The North British opened its branch to Kelso on 1 June 1851 and joined with the York, Newcastle & Berwick Railway's line from Tweedmouth at Sprouston Junction. The YN&BR, later to become part of the North Eastern system, had two stations in Scotland, at Sunilaws and Carham. The 3½ miles over the border operated by the NER was the only incidence of an English company operating inside Scotland. Stations from St Boswells were located at Maxton (3 miles), Rutherford (5½ miles), Roxburgh (8½ miles) and Kelso (11½ miles). The NBR provided six trains on weekdays and two on Sundays. The LNER operated six trains on weekdays with two extras on Saturdays. The passenger service was centred on Kelso with five trains running through to Berwick on weekdays only in the final years of the LNER. Under BR the passenger service was greatly reduced and Sprouston and Carham as well as the stations in England at Sunilaws, Twizell and Velvet Hall, were closed on 4 July 1955. BR only operated two trains from St Boswells through to Berwick on weekdays from that date although the St Boswells to Kelso section had five weekday trains with an extra on Saturdays. There was one through working from Kelso to Edinburgh via the Waverley route. The passenger service was withdrawn on 15 June 1964 and freight on 1 April 1968, the Kelso to Tweedmouth section being closed to all traffic on 29 March 1965. One of the features of the passenger working in the final years had been the one-coach train working through from Berwick with 'V1/V3' class 2-6-2Ts and subsequently Standard Class 2 2-6-0s in the '78000' series. Sunilaws and Carham are now private houses.

St Boswells in LNER days with a very traditional British freight train headed by 'F7' class 2-4-2T No 8301 built at Stratford in 1909 for the GER and withdrawn by the LNER in 1943. The LNER sent three 'F7s' to Scotland in 1931 and 1932 to work branch lines but the class was extinct by 1948. *Lens of Sutton*

Kelso with 'V1' class 2-6-2T No 67630 running bunker first with two LNER Thompson coaches. The engine was not rebuilt to a 'V3' and survived until December 1962 under BR. The train is the 4.5pm St Boswells to Berwick. Photograph taken on 6 May 1957. *Hugh Ballantyne*

Maxton station on 26 August 1960 on the Tweedmouth to St Boswells line sees a Gresley 'J39' class 0-6-0 with a coal train heading for St Boswells consisting of unfitted mineral wagons. An interesting feature here is the passing loop with concrete blocks instead of sleepers, probably put in during wartime. The Kelso to St Boswells section was closed to all traffic on and from 1 April 1968. *Hugh Ballantyne*

The imposing frontage of the former station at Selkirk on 4 April 1959 on the occasion of the BLS 'Scott Country' railtour. The passenger service was withdrawn on 10 September 1951 but freight traffic survived until 2 November 1964. *R. Hamilton*

The 'Scott Country' railtour headed by 'D34' class 4-4-0 No 62471 *Glen Falloch* at Lindean on the Selkirk branch. The engine was built at Cowlairs by the NBR in 1913 and was withdrawn by BR in 1960. *R. Hamilton*

Galashiels to Selkirk (6¼ miles)

The branch to Selkirk opened as the Selkirk Railway on 5 April 1856 under an Act of 1854 by the North British Railway. The passenger service consisted of 10 trains per day with an extra on Saturdays. There was a Sunday train which connected at Galashiels with the up and down Edinburgh train. Tourists came to Abbotsford Ferry (2¾ miles) to see the residence of Sir Walter Scott. The NBR provided a station at Lindean (4¼ miles) as well as at Selkirk

(6¼ miles). Abbotsford Ferry lasted until LNER days but was closed on 5 January 1931. The final year of operation by the LNER saw seven trains per weekday with two extras on Saturdays. The passenger service was withdrawn by BR on 10 September 1951, the freight from Selkirk to Netherdale Siding on 2 November 1964 and finally Netherdale Siding to Galashiels on 3 October 1966. The A7 road covers the old railway between Galashiels and Selkirk except the Lindean site.

A Scottish country station in a spotless condition during the LNER period prior to closure is seen at Lindean on the former Selkirk branch closed by BR in 1951. *Lens of Sutton*

St Boswells to Reston (30¼ miles)

The NBR opened a branch to Duns on 15 August 1849 (then spelt Dunse) under an Act of 1846. Dunse to Earlston opened on 16 November 1863 under the Berwickshire Railway Act of 1862. The final piece to Ravenswood Junction on the main line was completed by 2 October 1865 over the 19-arched Leaderfoot viaduct. The ambitions of the promoters were not fulfilled and there were only three through trains from Berwick to St Boswells with extras on Saturdays. Stations were located at Chirnside (4 miles), Edrom (5½ miles), Duns (8¾ miles), Marchmont (12½ miles), Greenlaw (16¼ miles), Gordon (20¼ miles) and Earlston (26¼ miles). At the Grouping the NBR was providing four trains from Berwick to St Boswells on weekdays, a service which the LNER perpetuated. Two short workings operated from Reston to Duns with connections to Edinburgh. Disaster struck the line on 12 August 1948 when flooding washed out the Greenlaw to Duns section and closed the line completely between those two points. The passenger service was also withdrawn from Greenlaw to St Boswells on the same occasion. Freight lasted until 19 July 1965 on the Greenlaw section and 7 November 1966 on the Reston to Duns section, where passenger trains had been withdrawn on 10 September 1951. The 'Scottish Rambler' railtour visited both open sections on 14 April 1963. Most of the stations are now private houses.

Right:
Chirnside on the Reston to Duns section of the former Dunse Railway with a Gresley 'J39' class 0-6-0 No 64843 and a very traditional mixed goods. The engine is coupled to an NER tender and classified as 'J39/3'. The signalman is about to hand over the token and stands on the NBR-type steps with a magnificent lower quadrant home signal dominating the scene. *W. S. Sellar*

Duns station on 14 April 1963 with the 'Scottish Rambler' railtour. The railway was opened in 1849 to Duns and extended to Earlston in 1863. The line was washed out from Duns to Greenlaw on 12 August 1948 and never reinstated. The Duns to Reston section survived under BR until 7 November 1966. *Author*

The 'Scottish Rambler' poses at Earlston on 14 April 1963 on the section of line that closed to all traffic on 19 July 1965. The 'B1' class 4-6-0 No 61324 has the class and shed allocation painted on the buffer beam as in LNER practice. *Author*

A Scotch mist hangs over Eyemouth where 'J39' class 0-6-0 No 64917 waits with a single Thompson coach for Burnmouth on 6 September 1958. LNER lamp standards support BR Scottish Region blue and enamel nameplates. The branch closed to all traffic on 5 February 1962. *Author*

Burnmouth to Eyemouth (3 miles)

The Eyemouth Railway branch to Burnmouth opened for traffic on 13 April 1891 under an Act of 1884 and was independent until absorbed into the NBR on 1 August 1900. The port developed into a seaside resort as well as a base for local fishing. The NBR ran through trains from Berwick and the LNER perpetuated this working. Out of the eight trains to use the branch on weekdays in 1947 there was still a through service operated by the LNER. The railway suffered severe damage with the storms of August 1948 and many people thought that the line would be closed as the viaduct over the Eye Water was affected. The branch was reopened on 29 June 1949 and the passenger service restored from that date. The final BR service consisted of four passenger trains per weekday which included the through working to Berwick. The branch was worked by LNER 'J39' 0-6-0s during its final years and was closed to all traffic on 5 February 1962.

Fountainhall Junction to Lauder (10½ miles)

The North British Waverley line passed through Fountainhall and was opened from Gorebridge to Bowland Bridge on 4 May 1848. The Lauder Light Railway Co was incorporated on 30 June 1898 as a light railway and opened on 2 July 1901. The line was operated by the NBR and absorbed into the LNER which provided three trains per weekday and an extra on Saturdays. Buses took the passenger traffic and the LNER withdrew the trains on 12 September 1932. Freight trains lasted longer and BR eventually withdrew them on 1 October 1958. The motive power was unusual in that the railway had steep gradients with tight curves and special engines had to be used. The NBR used 4-4-0 tanks (LNER Class D51), the LNER GER Class J69s and BR Class 2 2-6-0s in the '78000' series. The 'J69s' had to operate with half empty tanks and a tender, a most unusual arrangement for a British railway. The line had been opened in 1901 amid much public rejoicing and was closed with some ceremony with the running of the last train on 15 November 1958 organised by the Branch Line Society. The two-coach special left Fountainhall at 2pm and stopped at Oxton (6½ miles) for 10min. The station site at Lauder is now an industrial estate. A building survives at Oxton, probably the station house.

Below:
A scene on the Waverley as Standard Class 2 2-6-0 No 78049 approaches Fountainhall Junction with empty stock for the last train to Lauder. The Waverley route closed on 6 January 1969 but four examples of this class have survived into preservation. *Author*

Right:
An historic occasion was the running of the last train to Lauder on 15 November 1958 hauled by BR Standard Class 2 2-6-0 No 78049 seen here pulling up the bank out of Fountainhall Junction. The train consists of two bogie coaches which was the first time that such vehicles had been used on the branch. *Author*

Below right:
The last train has arrived at Lauder and large crowds have turned out for the occasion which was celebrated with a bun-fight in an adjacent marquee. The branch closed to passengers on 12 September 1932 and the station site is now an industrial estate. *Author*

Class J37 0-6-0 No 64614 heads a train of rails lifted from the Peebles branch of the Caledonian over the river into Peebles East on 14 November 1961. The Caley branch was closed in June 1950 but the connection to the former NBR line was used by freight trains until August 1959. *W. S. Sellar*

Hardengreen Junction to Galashiels (via Peebles) (37½ miles)

The Peebles Railway opened on 4 July 1855 and was incorporated by an Act of 8 July 1853 to run the 18¾ miles from Eskbank on the main line to Peebles. The line was leased to the NBR in 1861 which later absorbed it. The line was extended to join up with the direct Waverley route at Kilnknowe Junction on 18 June 1866. The NBR was connected with the Caledonian which had its own line to Peebles from Symington which opened on 1 February 1864. Stations were built at Bonnyrigg (9½ miles from Edinburgh), Hawthornden (11¼ miles), Rosslynlee (12½ miles), Pomathorn (15 miles), Leadburn (17½ miles), Eddleston (23 miles), Peebles (27 miles), Cardrona (30¼ miles), Innerleithen (33½ miles), Walkerburn (35¼ miles), Thornielee (38¾ miles) and Clovenfords (42¼ miles). Five through trains were run from Edinburgh to Galashiels via this route including a Peebles to Galashiels working on weekdays. Two Sunday trains also ran from Edinburgh to Peebles, one of which was extended to Innerleithen. The Sunday service had been discontinued by 1923 but the weekday trains had been increased to six each way with an extra on Saturdays. The LNER reduced the service to four

each way with an extra on Saturdays but BR increased the service and with dieselisation provided seven trains per weekday. BR opened a halt at Rosslynlee Hospital (13¼ miles) but closed Thornielee on 6 November 1950 and Leadburn on 7 March 1955. BR withdrew the passenger service on 5 February 1962 from Rosewell & Hawthornden (as Hawthornden had become under the LNER) to Galashiels, the Eskbank to Rosewell section lasting until 10 September 1962. The line was closed to all traffic from Rosewell to Kilnknowe Junction with the withdrawal of the passenger service. Freight traffic lasted until 27 March 1967 from Rosewell back to Hardengreen Junction. Clovenfords and Thornielee stations are now houses, Walkerburn has been demolished, Innerleithen is used as a store, Cardrona is in situ and Peebles has been obliterated by a new road. Eddleston was taken over and used by the Edinburgh Society of Model Engineers but is now a house. Leadburn's platforms have survived as a picnic spot where the nearby Leadburn Inn has a railway carriage restaurant. Pomathorn has been demolished but Rosslynlee is a house. At Rosewell & Hawthornden and Bonnyrigg the platforms survive as part of the walk leading to Penicuik and at Eskbank and Dalkeith the buildings survive intact.

Peebles West on 26 August 1960 after freight trains had ceased to run. The passenger service had been withdrawn on 5 June 1950, the station site is now a health centre. *Hugh Ballantyne*

Broughton on 14 October 1961 with ex-Caley 0-4-4T No 55124 shunting the stock of the 'Pentlands & Tinto' railtour. The engine of the CR '19' class was built at St Rollox in 1895 and survived until 1961. A CR 0-4-4T, No 419, has survived into preservation. *R. Hamilton*

Broughton was the principal station on the Caledonian line from Symington to Peebles and could boast three platforms in its heyday. The line closed to passengers on 5 June 1950 and freight on 7 June 1954. *Lens of Sutton*

Dolphinton Caledonian station had a through connection into the North British branch from Leadburn which had its own station in town. The branch from Carstairs was closed to passengers on 4 June 1945 and freight on 1 November 1950. *Lens of Sutton*

Symington to Peebles (19 miles)

The Symington, Biggar & Broughton Railway was incorporated on 21 May 1858 and opened on 5 November 1860. A further Act of 3 July 1860 authorised the construction of the line on to Peebles which was opened on 1 February 1864. The Caledonian amalgamated with the SB&BR on 1 August 1861. A short connection across the River Tweed was put in at Peebles to the NBR but no regular passenger service operated over it. The Caledonian was running six trains per weekday at Grouping but the LMS reduced the trains to four with a through coach to Glasgow. The stations were located at Coulter (2 miles), Biggar (3½ miles), Broughton (8 miles), Stobo (12½ miles), Lyne (16 miles) and Peebles (19 miles). BR withdrew the passenger service on 5 June 1950 and the freight back to Broughton on 7 June 1954. The connection at Peebles (West) and the NBR station was closed by BR on 1 August 1959, the Broughton to Symington section closing to freight on 4 April 1966. The Branch Line Society organised a special to Broughton on 14 October 1961 hauled by a Caledonian 0-4-4T, No 55124. The train was named the 'Pentlands & Tinto Express' and commemorated the named express service provided by the Caledonian from Edinburgh and Glasgow to Peebles and Moffat. Coulter is now an industrial site, Biggar is a road depot, Broughton and Lyne are houses, Stobo has been cleared and Peebles is now a health centre.

Leadburn to Dolphinton (10 miles)

The Leadburn, Linton & Dolphinton Railway opened on 1 July 1864 under an Act of 3 June 1862 and was worked by the NBR, being amalgamated with that company on 16 July 1866. There were stations at Lamancha (2¾ miles), Macbie Hill (4¼ miles) formerly Coalyburn, Broomlee (6½ miles) formerly West Linton, and Dolphinton (10 miles). Four trains per weekday were provided with an additional on Saturdays. The line was closed to all traffic by the LNER on 1 April 1933. Leadburn to Macbie Hill reopened for freight during World War 2 but was closed again by BR in December 1960.

Dunsyre on the Caledonian branch to Dolphinton was closed to passengers in 1945. The stationmaster poses on the platform with his family in far happier days when a railwayman's job was a job for life. *Lens of Sutton*

Carstairs to Dolphinton (11 miles)

A branch from Carstairs to Dolphinton was opened by the Caledonian on 1 March 1867 under its Act of 1863. A physical connection was made at Dolphinton with the North British branch from Leadburn. The CR and the NBR both had their own stations at Dolphinton, the NBR station being a dead-end terminal. The CR provided three trains per day on weekdays which had been reduced to one each way under the wartime LMS, which closed the branch on 4 June 1945 to passengers. BR withdrew the freight on 1 November 1950. There were stations at Bankhead (2 miles), Newbigging (4½ miles), Dunsyre (8½ miles) and Dolphinton (11 miles).

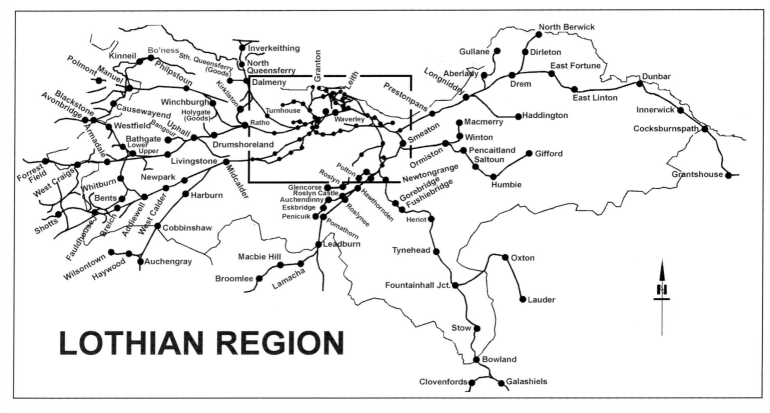

LOTHIAN REGION

The North British built a series of 0-4-0 saddle tanks at Cowlairs and classified them as 'G' class, later LNER 'Y9'. The first two engines in the class were built by Neilson & Co and the rest by NBR at Cowlairs. No 68100 built in 1899 lasted until 1960 under BR. The engines were used on the Leith Docks, Granton, Bonnington and South Leith branches in the Edinburgh area. No 68100 was one of the engines to be fitted with an additional tender. One example, No 68095, has been preserved. *Lens of Sutton*

Lothian

Edinburgh Suburban Lines

The North British Railway ran a circular service from Leith Central and back via Waverley, Gorgie and Portobello. The main line of the former Edinburgh & Glasgow Railway was opened on 21 February 1842 and originally terminated at Haymarket. The Waverley passenger station opened on 1 August 1846 and was known at the time as the General station. The circle line left the old E&G main line at Haymarket Central Junction and was authorised as the Edinburgh Suburban & Southside Railway in 1880 and 1882. The railway was a subsidiary of the NBR and amalgamated into that concern in 1885. The St Leonards branch was utilised from Duddingston Junction, the St Leonards line having been opened originally in 1831 as the Edinburgh & Dalkeith Railway. The E&DR opened its line to Leith South in 1838 with the NBR taking over the concern in 1845. The NBR modernised the E&DR, converted the gauge from 4ft 6in to standard and reintroduced a passenger service to St Leonards, Leith and Dalkeith in 1860. Patronage was light and the services were withdrawn on 30 September 1860. The St Leonards branch, noted for its 1 in 30 gradient, closed to the public on 1 November 1847 but continued to be used for goods until closed by BR on 5 August 1968. The NBR opened its Leith Central branch from Lochend Junction on 1 July 1903 and from here trains commenced their journey around the circle. BR withdrew the circular service on 10 September 1962 having closed Leith Central (since demolished) on 7 April 1952. On the circular service there were stations at

Piershill (1 mile from Leith Central), Portobello (2¼ miles), Duddingston (5 miles), Newington (6½ miles), Blackford Hill (7¼ miles), Morningside Road (8 miles), Craiglockhart (8¾ miles) and Gorgie (9¼ miles). Abbeyhill to Piershill and Portobello closed on 7 September 1964. Leith Central was converted into a diesel servicing depot and used until 1 May 1972. Leith South survives for freight train use and part of the St Leonards branch is now a footpath. The station buildings on the circle line have since been demolished but some platforms remain pending reopening.

The Edinburgh, Leith & Newhaven Railway was authorised on 13 August 1836 followed by another Act of 1 July 1839 which abandoned the Leith scheme. The terminus at the Edinburgh end was known as Canal Street with the lines through to Granton and Leith opening on 17 May 1847 as the Edinburgh, Leith & Granton Railway. Canal Street was at right angles to the Edinburgh & Glasgow terminus at North Street. The line went underground as a 1 in 27 gradient to Scotland Street where steam locomotives took over; a stationary engine hauled trains up the incline whilst trains downhill free-wheeled. An intensive service was provided initially but proved to be too frequent. The line eventually became part of the NBR system which joined up the Granton and Leith branches by building a direct line from Piershill Junction which opened for passengers on 22 March 1868. The NBR closed the Canal Street to Scotland Street section but Scotland St. Goods remained open until 6 November 1967. The Granton (NB) passenger service lasted until 2 November

No 49 *Gordon Highlander* stops for photographs at Gorgie on 16 October 1965 with a railtour special around the circle line at Edinburgh. BR withdrew the circular service on 10 September 1962 but the track is still in place pending possible reopening. *Author*

Above:
St Leonards was opened originally by the Edinburgh & Dalkeith Railway in 1831, later to become part of the North British. The line was noted for its severe gradient and survived as a goods only branch until 1968. Ex-NBR, LNER Class J35 No 64479 crosses the main road at Cairntows level crossing in October 1955. The engine was fitted with a tender cab by BR. *W. S. Sellar*

Right:
The St Leonards branch is worked by 'J35' class No 64486, built by the NBR in 1909 and withdrawn by BR in September 1958. The line terminated on the south side of the city and was the original terminus of the Edinburgh & Dalkeith Railway. *W. S. Sellar*

1925, the North Leith section surviving until 16 June 1947 under the LNER. Freight traffic had ceased by 2 December 1968 back to Bonnington South Junction but Powderhall is still in situ as waste trains run to the Edinburgh DC loading terminal.

In 1922 there were nine passenger trains per weekday from Waverley station to Granton calling at all stations to Trinity (3¼ miles from Edinburgh) and Granton NB (4½ miles). The North Leith trains consisted of 13 per day stopping at Abbeyhill (1¼ miles), Easter Road (1¾ miles, Leith Walk (2¼ miles), Bonnington (2¾ miles), Junction Road (3 miles) and North Leith (3¼ miles). The service was suspended during World War 1 and Powderhall closed permanently.

The Caledonian arrived in Edinburgh on 15 February 1848 and opened its Princes Street terminal on 2 May 1870. The terminus at Princes Street was rebuilt in 1894 followed by the Caledonian Hotel in 1903. The CR opened a line to Granton Harbour on 28 August 1861 and Leith on 1 September 1864, the passenger service being introduced on 1 August 1879. The CR built a branch to Seafield and South Leith Dock on

1 August 1903 and planned a passenger service which was never implemented. Platforms were built at Newhaven, Ferry Road and Leith Walk but were never used. On 1 March 1894 the CR opened the Barnton branch. Barnton was 5 miles from Princes Street and left the Leith branch at Craigleith. There was an intermediate station at Davidson's Mains, 1½ miles from Craigleith, and an approximately hourly service was provided on weekdays with two trains on Sundays. On the Caley Leith branch a half-hourly service was put on in the mornings and evenings with hourly trains for the rest of the day. The Caley built stations at Dalry Road (1¼ miles from Princes Street), Murrayfield (1½ miles), Craigleith (2¼ miles), Granton Road (4 miles), Newhaven (5 miles) and Leith (5½ miles).

On 1 December 1934 a station at East Pilton, 3½ miles from Princes Street, was opened. BR introduced multiple-unit diesels to work the Leith (North) ex-Caley branch in 1959 and a frequent service was provided but the new form of traction did not save the line, which was closed to passengers on 30 April 1962. The freight traffic to Leith Walk ceased from

Newhaven Junction on 4 January 1966. On the Barnton branch BR withdrew the passenger service on 7 May 1951 with freight back to Davidson's Mains. The Davidson's Mains to Craigleith freight was withdrawn from 1 June 1960. Dalry Road to Newhaven Junction was closed to freight on and from 4 September 1967 and Newhaven Junction to Leith (North) by 5 August 1968. All the ex-Caledonian lines in the Edinburgh area have now gone including the company's prestigious terminus at Princes Street, closed on 6 September 1965 and subsequently demolished. Trains on the ex-Caledonian main line now run into Waverley via Slateford Junction and Haymarket East Junction. The section from Slateford into Morrison Street Goods closed to freight traffic from 2 August 1966. Little remains to be seen today of the Caley branch lines in Edinburgh. Barnton has a newsagents on the site and Leith North is an industrial estate but the road-level buildings remain at Granton Road.

To the west of Edinburgh the North British opened a short branch in the suburbs to serve Corstorphine on 1 February 1902. The branch left the main line at Haymarket West Junction, serving Balgreen Halt (1¼ miles from the terminus) and Pinkhill (¾ mile) before arriving at the terminus which was 1½ miles from the junction. Passenger trains were frequent throughout the day and could be worked by any form of motive power as engines usually did a 'filling in' turn from Waverley. The appearance of Gresley Pacifics on such trains was not uncommon. The passenger service was withdrawn on 1 January 1968 and the line closed to all traffic after 5 February 1968. At the other end of the city the NBR had a short branch from Newhailes Junction to Musselburgh, a distance of 1½ miles. The branch was opened as early as 16 July 1847, being an offshoot of the Edinburgh & Dalkeith Fisherrow branch of 1831 which the NBR inherited. The passenger service to Musselburgh was withdrawn on 7 September 1964 but freight lasted until 6 September 1971. Musselburgh to Fisherrow branch junction is now covered by a road for a distance of half a mile. Corstorphine station site is now occupied by a housing estate.

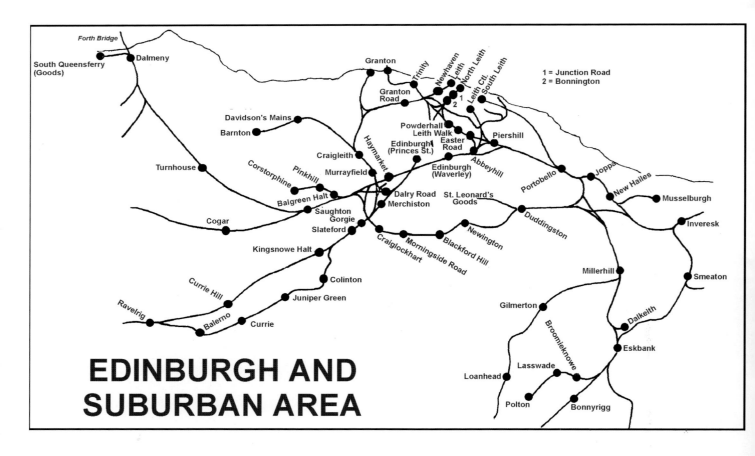

EDINBURGH AND SUBURBAN AREA

Above:
No 67649 at Bonnington with a van train from Leith on 4 August 1959. The engine was built at Doncaster in December 1935 and was one of Gresley's 'V1' class three-cylinder 2-6-2Ts that was not rebuilt to a 'V3' (the difference being increased boiler pressure). A total of 92 engines were built and the class could be found in the North East as well as Scotland. No 67649 lasted until July 1962 but no member of the class has survived. *W. S. Sellar*

Above right:
No 64947, a Gresley 'J39' 0-6-0, shunts at Leith North on 4 March 1960. The branch was closed to passengers on 16 June 1947 by the LNER, having been closed during World War 1 by the NBR. *W. S. Sellar*

Right:
Granton Harbour with 'C16' class 4-4-2T No 67492 working an SLS special over the Duke of Buccleuch line on 6 September 1958. The 'C16' class, built between 1915 and 1921, totalled a class of 21 engines and were known as 'L' class under the NBR. The engine dated from 1916 and lasted until 1960 under BR. The class was extinct by 1961, no examples having survived. *Author*

Corstorphine was a suburban terminus only 1½ miles from the junction which the NBR opened on 1 February 1902 and BR closed on 5 February 1968. In steam days the line was used by main line engines on 'filling in' turns from Haymarket. Gresley 'A3' class 4-6-2 No 60060 *The Tetrarch* is seen on suburban stock on 15 June 1963. The engine was built in 1925, fitted with double chimney in 1959 and withdrawn in September 1963. *W. S. Sellar*

Caley 0-6-0 No 57654 shunts at Davidson's Mains on the Barnton CR branch closed to passengers on 7 May 1951. Freight was withdrawn on 1 June 1960 back to Craigleith on the former Leith (CR) branch. *W. S. Sellar*

The Musselburgh branch was 1½ miles long and dated from 1847. The line was closed to passengers on 7 September 1964 and freight on 6 September 1971. Gresley 'V3' class 2-6-2T No 67609 waits with an Edinburgh Waverley train on 29 May 1958. Part of the branch is now covered by a road. *W. S. Sellar*

Millerhill to Glencorse (8 miles)

The Edinburgh, Loanhead & Roslin Railway was authorised on 20 June 1870 and opened on 23 July 1874. The line was extended to Glencorse on 2 July 1977 and became part of the NBR on 1 August of that year. The branch served collieries in the area and these provided lucrative traffic for the railway. The NBR provided five passenger trains on weekdays with two extras on Saturdays. A through service to Edinburgh was run which continued until the LNER closed the line to passengers on 1 May 1933. BR closed the line to freight from 1 July 1959 back to Roslin and on 1 June 1969 back to Bilston Glen Colliery. Millerhill Junction to Bilston Glen Colliery closed to all traffic on 5 June 1989 but reopened in May 1991 to remove coal to Cockenzie Power Station. The line could be reopened to passengers in the future. Passenger stations were located at Roslin (2 miles from Glencorse), Loanhead (3¾ miles) and Gilmerton (5¼ miles). The Branch Line Society railtour visited the line on 16 October 1965. Glencorse buildings have been removed, Roslin burnt down on 3 May 1959 and Loanhead is still in situ.

Glenesk Junction to Dalkeith (½ mile)

The branch was originally part of the 4ft 6in gauge Edinburgh & Dalkeith Railway of 1838, later to be purchased by the NBR which modernised the line and changed the gauge to standard. The NBR reopened the line on 14 July 1847 and provided eight trains per weekday until World War 1 but only two at Grouping. The LNER withdrew the passenger trains on 5 January 1942 but freight traffic under BR ceased after 10 August 1964. The station site is a bus garage and the old trackbed from Glenesk Junction is now a footpath.

'J35' class 0-6-0 No 64479 shunts the goods at Dalkeith on 21 April 1960, an early terminus of the Edinburgh & Dalkeith Railway of 1831. The 'J35' was built at Cowlairs in 1908 and withdrawn by BR in 1961. *W. S. Sellar*

Lasswade viaduct on the Polton branch with a 'J35' class 0-6-0 on the branch goods. No 64479, built at Cowlairs by the NBR in 1908, survived until December 1961 under BR. *W. S. Sellar*

Ex-NBR No 65344 shunts at Polton on 20 May 1960. The engine was built in December 1900 at Cowlairs and withdrawn by BR in November 1962. Another member of the 'J36' class, No 65243, has survived and can be seen on the Bo'ness & Kinneil Railway. The branch closed to passengers on 10 September 1951. *W. S. Sellar*

Esk Valley Junction to Polton (1½ miles)

The Esk Valley Railway was opened to Polton on 15 April 1867, having been leased to the North British under its Act of 1866. Seven trains were run on weekdays and two extras on Saturdays. There were stations at Lasswade (1 mile from Polton), and Broomieknowe (1½ miles). A through passenger service was run from Edinburgh Waverley but the LNER reduced the trains to five per day. BR withdrew the passenger trains on 10 September 1951 and freight on 18 May 1964. At Polton the station house survives but the rest of the site has been built over. Lasswade is now a housing estate and Broomieknowe has disappeared but a footpath extends from here to Hardengreen Junction.

Rosewell & Hawthornden to Penicuik (4½ miles)

This branch was opened to passengers as the Penicuik Railway on 2 September 1872 and worked by the North British which provided five trains per weekday to Edinburgh with two extras on Saturdays. There were stations at Eskbridge (¾ mile from Penicuik), Auchendinny (1¼ miles) and Rosslyn Castle (3 miles). The LNER reduced the passenger service to four weekday trains with an extra on Saturdays by 1947 and BR closed the line along with the Polton service on 10 September 1951. Freight trains ran until 27 March 1967 and today most of the trackbed is now a footpath. Penicuik station was incorporated into a mill but has since been cleared. Eskbridge has disappeared and at Auchendinny and Rosslyn Castle the platforms are intact.

Smeaton to Macmerry (6¾ miles)

The line from Monktonhall Junction to Smeaton opened to mineral traffic in December 1866 and was extended to Ormiston on 1 May 1867. The Macmerry branch was opened to passengers on 1 July 1872 when a through service was provided by the NBR from Edinburgh Waverley. There were intermediate stations at Smeaton (7¾ miles from Waverley), Ormiston (11¾ miles), Winton (13 miles) and Macmerry (14¼ miles). The NBR did not provide much of a service, there being only two trains per weekday with an extra on Saturdays. The LNER withdrew the passenger service on 1 July 1925 and BR the freight on 2 May 1960. The SLS visited the line with a railtour on 6 September 1958 comprising an ex-NBR 'C16' class 4-4-2T and Gresley stock. Ormiston station has been demolished but the platforms provide a picnic site for walks on the Pencaitland Railway Walk which runs from Smeaton to Saltoun. Macmerry station site has been cleared.

Ormiston to Gifford (9¼ miles)

On 14 October 1901 the Gifford Light Railway was opened from Ormiston Junction with passenger stations at Pencaitland (2 miles), Saltoun (3½ miles), Humbie (5½ miles) and Gifford (9¼ miles). The stations were of a light construction and the railway was leased and worked by the North British. Engines used were the NBR 'D51' class 4-4-0T and later the 'J24' class 0-6-0T. There were three trains per weekday with an extra on Saturdays with through working or a connection to Edinburgh. The LNER withdrew the passenger service on 3 April 1933 and BR withdrew the freight in August 1948 back to Humbie, on 2 May 1960 back to Saltoun and 24 May 1965 back to Smeaton. The Pencaitland Railway Walk runs to Saltoun and at Gifford a bungalow named 'Buffers' has been built on the site. Humbie station and goods platforms survive, Saltoun has been demolished and at Pencaitland there is only a mound to mark the spot, as at Ormiston and Smeaton.

Below:
A final view of the rather overgrown platform at Macmerry on 6 September 1958 as the SLS special steams out with the last passenger train. The regular passenger service was withdrawn as early as 1 July 1925 with freight surviving until 2 May 1960 under BR. *Author*

Above right:
Ormiston with the Saltoun goods arriving on 4 March 1960 headed by Ivatt Class 2 2-6-0 No 46462. The station was originally the junction for the Ormiston to Gifford branch of the former Gifford Light Railway opened to the public on 14 October 1901. *W. S. Sellar*

Below right:
Saltoun was an intermediate station on the goods only branch to Humbie when this photograph was taken on 4 March 1960. The line was cut back to Saltoun on 2 May 1960 and Smeaton on 24 May 1965. *W. S. Sellar*

Haddington was a 4¾-mile branch of the former NBR opened in 1846 and closed to passengers by BR on 5 December 1949. The RCTS/SLS special is seen at the terminus on 11 June 1960 with 'J35' class 0-6-0 No 64489 of 1909. The branch closed to freight traffic on 1 April 1968. *Author*

North Berwick with 'V1' class 2-6-2T No 67659 on a train of Gresley suburban stock on 1 May 1954. The branch is still open for passenger traffic and has a regular service to Edinburgh. *W. A. C. Smith*

LMS-built 0-4-4T No 55260 passes Colinton with the SLS/RCTS tour on 20 June 1962. The Balerno branch of the former Caledonian Railway was closed to passengers on 1 November 1943 by the LMS. *R. Hamilton*

Longniddry to Haddington (4¾ miles)

The North British Railway was authorised on 4 July 1844 from Edinburgh to Berwick with a branch to Haddington. The main line and the branch opened for passengers on 18 June 1846. The NBR provided 10 trains per day with an extra on Fridays and two extras on Saturdays. There were even two trains on Sundays, a service that lasted through LNER days into Nationalisation. BR withdrew the passenger trains on 5 December 1949 and freight on 1 April 1968. The old trackbed is now a footpath but the station at Haddington has been demolished.

Aberlady Junction to Gullane (4¾ miles)

The Aberlady, Gullane & North Berwick Railway was promoted as an independent concern to join up with the North British branch but got as far as Gullane. The railway was taken over by the NBR in 1890 and opened on 1 April 1898. The passenger service consisted of eight trains per weekday including through trains from Edinburgh. The branch had a named train, the 'Lothian Coast Express' which had portions from North Berwick and Dunbar as well as Gullane for Edinburgh. The LNER closed the line to passengers on 12 September 1932 and BR ceased to operate freight after 15 June 1964. There was an intermediate private golfers' halt at Luffress and a station at Aberlady, 3 miles from Gullane.

Drem to North Berwick (4¾ miles)

The line was opened on 17 June 1850 under an Act of 1846.

There were nine trains per weekday under the NBR including the named 'Lothian Coast Express'. An intermediate station was opened at Dirleton, 2½ miles from Drem. Unlike the other coastal branches the North Berwick line has survived and is today part of the ScotRail network. The LNER ran 14 trains per weekday, BR 16 and ScotRail runs 18. ScotRail even runs five trains on Sundays. The intermediate at Dirleton closed on 1 February 1954.

Slateford to Balerno (5 miles)

The branch was authorised on 20 June 1860 and opened on 1 August 1874 by the Caledonian. There were intermediate stations at Colinton (1½ miles), Juniper Green (2½ miles) and Currie (3¾ miles). The CR ran a frequent service of 16 trains per weekday to Princes Street. The LMS opened a halt at Hailes, between Colinton and Slateford, on 26 September 1927 to cater for golfers. A special class of 0-4-4T engine was built for this branch and the Cathcart Circle line known as 'Balerno Tanks'. The LMS withdrew the passenger trains on 1 November 1943 which was an LMS 'service suspended' arrangement, the railway company not admitting to closure as such. BR gave an official date of 13 June 1949 and ran freight traffic until 4 December 1967. The line was connected to the main line at Ravelrig Junction which was closed after 9 September 1963. The railway is now a footpath known as the Waters of Leith Walkway and the platform with the tunnel survives at Juniper Green. Colinton has been built over and Balerno has been demolished.

Standard 2-6-0 No 78046 works tender first on the ex-Caledonian Balerno branch on 19 April 1965. The two preserved Caley coaches are in tow on the branch and by BR to freight on 4 December 1967. Most of the old trackbed has been converted into a walk known as 'The Waters of Leith Walkway'. *Author*

A view taken at Kirkliston in LNER days prior to closure. The line closed to regular passenger traffic on 22 September 1930 and freight on 7 February 1966. The trackbed is now a footpath. *Lens of Sutton*

North British 'J37' 0-6-0 No 64603 poses at South Queensferry with the 'Scottish Rambler' on 13 April 1963. The engine was built at Cowlairs in November 1919 as an NBR 'S' class and withdrawn by BR in December 1963. The branch closed to passengers in 1929 and to freight in 1967. *Author*

Ratho to Dalmeny (via Kirkliston) (7 miles)

The North British provided a passenger service of five trains per weekday to Dalmeny via Kirkliston and two per weekday to South Queensferry via Kirkliston in its 1922 timetable. The NBR opened the line from Ratho through Kirkliston to Dalmeny on 1 March 1866 and extended the branch to South Queensferry on 1 June 1868. The line to Port Edgar from South Queensferry opened on 1 October 1878. When the Forth Bridge opened in 1890 the South Queensferry branch was of less importance but passenger trains ran until 14 January 1929 and freight traffic survived until 6 November 1967. The passenger service from Ratho to Dalmeny was withdrawn by the LNER on 22 September 1930 and freight through Kirkliston on 7 February 1966. The Dalmeny to Ratho trackbed through Kirkliston is now a footpath. South Queensferry has now disappeared.

Uphall to Bangour (2 miles)

A private railway known as the Bangour Hospital Railway ran from Uphall on the NBR Bathgate line to Bangour Mental Hospital to take passengers to the hospital. The line was opened on 19 June 1905 and worked by the NBR under a 1900 Act. The railway was staffed by NBR personnel, the tickets being issued to Bangour Private. Visitors, patients and staff used the railway which had an intermediate station at Dechmont (1½ miles) where the staff resided. The line was closed after World War 1 and is shown in the 1922 *Bradshaw* as 'service suspended'. There were four trains per weekday so presumably there were no Sunday visiting hours at the hospital.

Bathgate with 'J35' class No 64468 on 31 December 1955 shortly before closure of the passenger service to Airdrie and Edinburgh. The engine was built by the North British Locomotive Co in 1906 and withdrawn by BR in 1960. The passenger service from Edinburgh was recently reinstated by BR. *W. S. Sellar*

'J36' class 0-6-0 No 65261, seen shunting at Addiewell on 30 October 1960, did not have a vacuum brake pipe on the front buffer beam. The engine was built by Sharp, Stewart in 1892 and survived until October 1962. The line closed to all traffic on 24 April 1963. *W. S. Sellar*

Ratho to Bathgate (10½ miles)

Passenger trains now run to Bathgate where an hourly service operates every day of the week to Edinburgh. The NBR used the Bathgate route for its alternative Edinburgh to Glasgow service which was run down by the LNER and BR which withdrew the passenger service on 8 January 1956. The line had been opened as the Edinburgh & Bathgate Railway on 12 November 1849 and extended as the Bathgate & Coatbridge Railway on 11 August 1862. The NBR ran a through service from 1 April 1871.

Auchengray to Wilsontown (3½ miles)

The Caledonian Railway received authorisation under an Act of 21 July 1859 to construct a branch of 2¾ miles from the main line at Wilsontown Junction. The branch was opened in 1870 to serve coal mines and ironworks and had a triangular junction with the CR main line. Passenger trains left from a bay platform at Auchengray and diverged on to the branch ½-mile from the station. Seven passenger trains were run on weekdays with two extras on Saturdays. There was an intermediate station at Haywood, 2 miles from Auchengray. The line extended beyond Wilsontown to Kingshill Colliery, a distance of 3¼ miles. BR withdrew the passenger service on 10 September 1951 and the freight on 4 May 1964. The station site at Wilsontown has now been cleared.

Avonbridge with 'J36' class 0-6-0 No 65281 with a brake van on 26 December 1960. The engine, dating from 1896 and built at Cowlairs in the NBR works, only had six months to go to withdrawal in July 1961. Blackston to Avonbridge closed to all traffic on 28 December 1964. *W. S. Sellar*

Wilsontown signalbox with Caley 0-6-0 No 57670 on the daily goods. The passenger service was withdrawn on 10 September 1951 and the freight on 4 May 1964. *W. S. Sellar*

Bibliography and Acknowledgements

A History of the Great North of Scotland Railway, Sir Malcolm Barclay Harvey (LPC 1949 Reprinted Ian Allan 1998)

SLS/RCTS Scottish Railtour Itinerary, W. A. Camwell (SLS 1960)

British Branch Lines, H. A. Vallance (Batsford 1965)

The Glasgow & South Western Railway, Campbell Highet (Oakwood 1965)

Bradshaw's 1910 Railway Guide (reprint), David St John Thomas (D&C 1968)

Locomotives of the LNER Parts 1 to 9, E. V. Fry (RCTS 1968)

Bradshaw's Railway Manual & Shareholders' Guide (reprint), R. W. Clinker (D&C 1968)

The Highland Railway, H. A. Vallance (D&C 1969)

British Steam Railcars, R. W. Rush (Oakwood 1969)

The West Highland Railway, David St John Thomas (D&C 1970)

The Light Railway Handbook, R. W. Kidner (Oakwood 1971)

Little & Good, The GNSRA Committee (SLS 1972)

Locomotives at the Grouping, H. C. Casserley & S. W. Johnston (Ian Allan 1974)

Walking Old Railways, G. Somerville (D&C 1979)

A Guide to the Steam Railways of Britain, Awdry/Cook (Pelham 1979)

Forgotten Railways Scotland, David St John Thomas (D&C 1981)

The Story & Tales of the Buchan Line, Alan H. Sangster (OPC 1983)

Regional History of the Railways of Great Britain Vol 6, David St John Thomas (D&C 1984)

Railway Rights of Way, R. Ellis (BLS 1985)

Bradshaw's 1922 Railway Guide (reprint), David St John Thomas (D&C 1985)

Register of Closed Railways 1948-1991, G. Hirst (Milepost 1991)

Regional History of the Railways of Great Britain Vol 15, David St John Thomas (D&C 1993)

The Directory of Railway Stations, R. V. J. Butt (PSL 1995)

Rail Atlas of Great Britain & Ireland, S. K. Baker (OPC 1996)

Tayside's Railway Dundee & Perth, W. A. C. Smith & Paul Andrews (Irwell 1997)

Vinters Gazetteer 1997-1998, Jeff Vinter (Crosswave 1997)

The author and publisher would also like to acknowledge the assistance of Keith Jones and the GNSRA, W. A. C. Smith, Roy Hamilton, Fred Pugh, Nick Tindall, J. Jervis, K. Fenwick, *Railway Magazine, Steam Days, British Railway Journal, Railway World*, and Mike Pain for drawing the maps.

Index